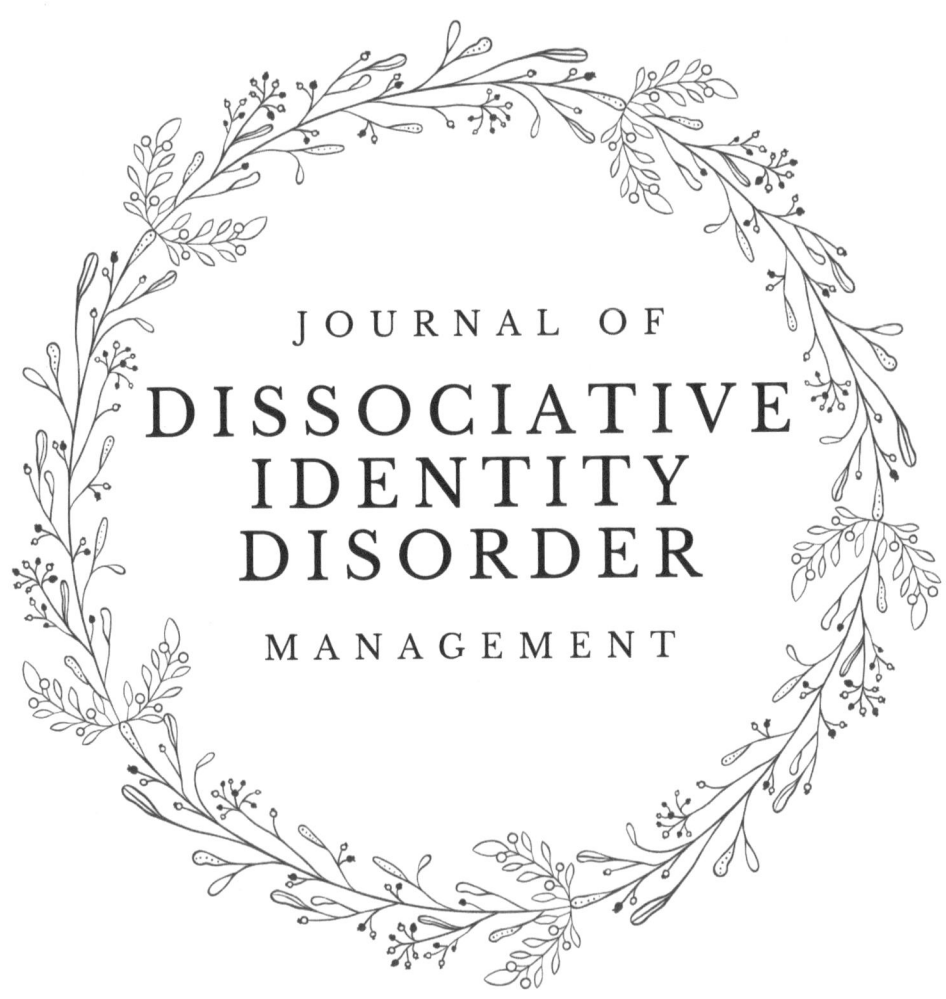

JOURNAL OF DISSOCIATIVE IDENTITY DISORDER MANAGEMENT

PAGES 2 - 3   SYSTEM RULES

PAGES 4 - 18   ALTER CHECK-IN (NOTE TIME AND SWITCH TRIGGER + NOTES)

PAGES 19 - 59   ALTER INTRODUCTION AND PROFILE PAGES

PAGES 60 - 82   SYSTEM MAP PAGES

PAGES 83 - 107 GRATITUDE PROMPTS & INSPIRATIONAL QUOTES W. ILLUSTRATIONS TO COLOR IN!

PAGES 107 - 210 DID SYMPTOM TRACKER, MOOD VS ENERGY LOG AND LINED JOURNAL PAGES

This journal is to help support mental health of the system in a non judgemental way that allows for both plurals and integration (but does not pressure! its just flexible!). This book allows for 50 alter introductions (someone can put more on the journal pages). It has system map pages as well as an alter check in where they can track switch triggers, notes (helps when things are misplaced) and plenty of mood trackers as well as journal pages to communicate with alters.

Write down thoughts and feelings, system rules, therapy notes, to-do lists, and more. With weekly energy and mood journals and symptom trackers.

This journal also has gratitude prompts and inspirational quotes to encourage self-care and a positive mindset. To help refocus bad days and remember why life is GREAT!

This book is also a journal with many lined pages in this journal your thoughts and track achievements on the lined pages.

System Rules

WRITE DOWN THE RULES FOR THIS DIARY AND ALSO YOUR SYSTEM RULES FOR BEHAVIOUR, DECISION MAKING ATTENDING THERAPY AND MORE.

System Rules

WRITE DOWN THE RULES FOR THIS DIARY AND ALSO YOUR SYSTEM RULES FOR BEHAVIOUR, DECISION MAKING ATTENDING THERAPY AND MORE.

ALTER CHECK - IN

WRITE DOWN TIME OF SWITCH, TRIGGER REASON, DURATION AND ANY NOTES TO COMMUNICATE TO THE OTHER ALTERS

ALTER NAME	SWITCH START TIME	DURATION	DATE	NOTES & SWITCH TRIGGER

ALTER CHECK - IN

WRITE DOWN TIME OF SWITCH, TRIGGER REASON, DURATION AND ANY NOTES TO COMMUNICATE TO THE OTHER ALTERS

ALTER NAME	SWITCH START TIME	DURATION	DATE	NOTES & SWITCH TRIGGER

ALTER CHECK - IN

WRITE DOWN TIME OF SWITCH, TRIGGER REASON, DURATION AND ANY NOTES TO COMMUNICATE TO THE OTHER ALTERS

ALTER NAME	SWITCH START TIME	DURATION	DATE	NOTES & SWITCH TRIGGER

ALTER CHECK - IN

WRITE DOWN TIME OF SWITCH, TRIGGER REASON, DURATION AND ANY NOTES TO COMMUNICATE TO THE OTHER ALTERS

ALTER NAME	SWITCH START TIME	DURATION	DATE	NOTES & SWITCH TRIGGER

ALTER CHECK - IN

WRITE DOWN TIME OF SWITCH, TRIGGER REASON, DURATION AND ANY NOTES TO COMMUNICATE TO THE OTHER ALTERS

ALTER NAME	SWITCH START TIME	DURATION	DATE	NOTES & SWITCH TRIGGER

ALTER CHECK - IN

WRITE DOWN TIME OF SWITCH, TRIGGER REASON, DURATION AND ANY NOTES TO COMMUNICATE TO THE OTHER ALTERS

ALTER NAME	SWITCH START TIME	DURATION	DATE	NOTES & SWITCH TRIGGER

ALTER CHECK - IN

WRITE DOWN TIME OF SWITCH, TRIGGER REASON, DURATION AND ANY NOTES TO COMMUNICATE TO THE OTHER ALTERS

ALTER NAME	SWITCH START TIME	DURATION	DATE	NOTES & SWITCH TRIGGER

ALTER CHECK - IN

WRITE DOWN TIME OF SWITCH, TRIGGER REASON, DURATION AND ANY NOTES TO COMMUNICATE TO THE OTHER ALTERS

ALTER NAME	SWITCH START TIME	DURATION	DATE	NOTES & SWITCH TRIGGER

ALTER CHECK - IN

WRITE DOWN TIME OF SWITCH, TRIGGER REASON, DURATION AND ANY NOTES TO COMMUNICATE TO THE OTHER ALTERS

ALTER NAME	SWITCH START TIME	DURATION	DATE	NOTES & SWITCH TRIGGER

ALTER CHECK - IN

WRITE DOWN TIME OF SWITCH, TRIGGER REASON, DURATION AND ANY NOTES TO COMMUNICATE TO THE OTHER ALTERS

ALTER NAME	SWITCH START TIME	DURATION	DATE	NOTES & SWITCH TRIGGER

ALTER CHECK - IN

WRITE DOWN TIME OF SWITCH, TRIGGER REASON, DURATION AND ANY NOTES TO COMMUNICATE TO THE OTHER ALTERS

ALTER NAME	SWITCH START TIME	DURATION	DATE	NOTES & SWITCH TRIGGER

ALTER CHECK - IN

WRITE DOWN TIME OF SWITCH, TRIGGER REASON, DURATION AND ANY NOTES TO COMMUNICATE TO THE OTHER ALTERS

ALTER NAME	SWITCH START TIME	DURATION	DATE	NOTES & SWITCH TRIGGER

ALTER CHECK - IN

WRITE DOWN TIME OF SWITCH, TRIGGER REASON, DURATION AND ANY NOTES TO COMMUNICATE TO THE OTHER ALTERS

ALTER NAME	SWITCH START TIME	DURATION	DATE	NOTES & SWITCH TRIGGER

ALTER CHECK - IN

WRITE DOWN TIME OF SWITCH, TRIGGER REASON, DURATION AND ANY NOTES TO COMMUNICATE TO THE OTHER ALTERS

ALTER NAME	SWITCH START TIME	DURATION	DATE	NOTES & SWITCH TRIGGER

ALTER CHECK - IN

WRITE DOWN TIME OF SWITCH, TRIGGER REASON, DURATION AND ANY NOTES TO COMMUNICATE TO THE OTHER ALTERS

ALTER NAME	SWITCH START TIME	DURATION	DATE	NOTES & SWITCH TRIGGER

MEMBERS INTRODUCTION & PROFILE

USE THESE PROFILES TO INTRODUCE YOURSELF AND FOR OTHER NEW ALTERS TO USE TO INTRODUCE THEMSELVES TO THE REST OF YOUR SYSTEM AND LEARN MORE ABOUT THEM. THESE ARE JUST PROMPTS THAT MAY NOT BE RELEVANT AND YOU CAN PUT MORE DETAILED EXPLAINATIONS IN YOUR NOTE SECTIONS INSTEAD.

NAME OF ALTER: _____

AGE: _____

BIRTHDAY: _____

GENDER IDENTITY: _____

SEXUALITY PREFERENCE (E.G. LGBTQ STRAIGHT ETC):
_____

LIKES:
_____
_____
_____
_____

DISLIKES:
_____
_____
_____
_____

RELEVANT CATEGORIZATIONS

| HOST/ANP | INTERNAL HELPER | TEEN ALTER | OPPOSITE SEX ALTER | LITTLE |
| INTROJECT | PROTECTOR | EMOTIONAL | FRAGMENT | LOCKED | PERSECUTOR |

OTHER _____

NOTES: _____
_____
_____
_____
_____
_____
_____

MEMBERS INTRODUCTION & PROFILE

USE THESE PROFILES TO INTRODUCE YOURSELF AND FOR OTHER NEW ALTERS TO USE TO INTRODUCE THEMSELVES TO THE REST OF YOUR SYSTEM AND LEARN MORE ABOUT THEM. THESE ARE JUST PROMPTS THAT MAY NOT BE RELEVANT AND YOU CAN PUT MORE DETAILED EXPLAINATIONS IN YOUR NOTE SECTIONS INSTEAD.

NAME OF ALTER: _____

AGE: _____

BIRTHDAY: _____

GENDER IDENTITY: _____

SEXUALITY PREFERENCE (E.G. LGBTQ STRAIGHT ETC):
_____

LIKES:
_____
_____
_____
_____

DISLIKES:
_____
_____
_____
_____

RELEVANT CATEGORIZATIONS

HOST/ANP   INTERNAL HELPER   TEEN ALTER   OPPOSITE SEX ALTER   LITTLE
INTROJECT   PROTECTOR   EMOTIONAL   FRAGMENT   LOCKED   PERSECUTOR
OTHER_____

NOTES: _____
_____
_____
_____
_____
_____
_____

MEMBERS INTRODUCTION & PROFILE

USE THESE PROFILES TO INTRODUCE YOURSELF AND FOR OTHER NEW ALTERS TO USE TO INTRODUCE THEMSELVES TO THE REST OF YOUR SYSTEM AND LEARN MORE ABOUT THEM. THESE ARE JUST PROMPTS THAT MAY NOT BE RELEVANT AND YOU CAN PUT MORE DETAILED EXPLAINATIONS IN YOUR NOTE SECTIONS INSTEAD.

NAME OF ALTER: _____

AGE: _____

BIRTHDAY: _____

GENDER IDENTITY: _____

SEXUALITY PREFERENCE (E.G. LGBTQ STRAIGHT ETC): _____

LIKES:
_____
_____
_____
_____

DISLIKES:
_____
_____
_____
_____

RELEVANT CATEGORIZATIONS

HOST/ANP   INTERNAL HELPER   TEEN ALTER   OPPOSITE SEX ALTER   LITTLE

INTROJECT   PROTECTOR   EMOTIONAL   FRAGMENT   LOCKED   PERSECUTOR

OTHER _____

NOTES: _____
_____
_____
_____
_____
_____
_____

MEMBERS INTRODUCTION & PROFILE

USE THESE PROFILES TO INTRODUCE YOURSELF AND FOR OTHER NEW ALTERS TO USE TO INTRODUCE THEMSELVES TO THE REST OF YOUR SYSTEM AND LEARN MORE ABOUT THEM. THESE ARE JUST PROMPTS THAT MAY NOT BE RELEVANT AND YOU CAN PUT MORE DETAILED EXPLAINATIONS IN YOUR NOTE SECTIONS INSTEAD.

NAME OF ALTER: _____

AGE: _____

BIRTHDAY: _____

GENDER IDENTITY: _____

SEXUALITY PREFERENCE (E.G. LGBTQ STRAIGHT ETC):
_____

LIKES:
_____
_____
_____
_____

DISLIKES:
_____
_____
_____
_____

RELEVANT CATEGORIZATIONS

HOST/ANP   INTERNAL HELPER   TEEN ALTER   OPPOSITE SEX ALTER   LITTLE
INTROJECT   PROTECTOR   EMOTIONAL   FRAGMENT   LOCKED   PERSECUTOR
OTHER _____

NOTES: _____
_____
_____
_____
_____
_____
_____

MEMBERS INTRODUCTION & PROFILE

USE THESE PROFILES TO INTRODUCE YOURSELF AND FOR OTHER NEW ALTERS TO USE TO INTRODUCE THEMSELVES TO THE REST OF YOUR SYSTEM AND LEARN MORE ABOUT THEM. THESE ARE JUST PROMPTS THAT MAY NOT BE RELEVANT AND YOU CAN PUT MORE DETAILED EXPLAINATIONS IN YOUR NOTE SECTIONS INSTEAD.

NAME OF ALTER: _____

AGE: _____

BIRTHDAY: _____

GENDER IDENTITY: _____

SEXUALITY PREFERENCE (E.G. LGBTQ STRAIGHT ETC):
_____

LIKES:
_____
_____
_____
_____

DISLIKES:
_____
_____
_____
_____

RELEVANT CATEGORIZATIONS

| HOST/ANP | INTERNAL HELPER | TEEN ALTER | OPPOSITE SEX ALTER | LITTLE |
| INTROJECT | PROTECTOR | EMOTIONAL | FRAGMENT | LOCKED | PERSECUTOR |

OTHER _____

NOTES: _____
_____
_____
_____
_____
_____
_____

MEMBERS INTRODUCTION & PROFILE

USE THESE PROFILES TO INTRODUCE YOURSELF AND FOR OTHER NEW ALTERS TO USE TO INTRODUCE THEMSELVES TO THE REST OF YOUR SYSTEM AND LEARN MORE ABOUT THEM. THESE ARE JUST PROMPTS THAT MAY NOT BE RELEVANT AND YOU CAN PUT MORE DETAILED EXPLAINATIONS IN YOUR NOTE SECTIONS INSTEAD.

NAME OF ALTER: _____

AGE: _____

BIRTHDAY: _____

GENDER IDENTITY: _____

SEXUALITY PREFERENCE (E.G. LGBTQ STRAIGHT ETC):
_____

LIKES:
_____
_____
_____
_____

DISLIKES:
_____
_____
_____
_____

RELEVANT CATEGORIZATIONS

| HOST/ANP | INTERNAL HELPER | TEEN ALTER | OPPOSITE SEX ALTER | LITTLE |
| INTROJECT | PROTECTOR | EMOTIONAL | FRAGMENT | LOCKED | PERSECUTOR |

OTHER_____

NOTES: _____
_____
_____
_____
_____
_____
_____

MEMBERS INTRODUCTION & PROFILE

USE THESE PROFILES TO INTRODUCE YOURSELF AND FOR OTHER NEW ALTERS TO USE TO INTRODUCE THEMSELVES TO THE REST OF YOUR SYSTEM AND LEARN MORE ABOUT THEM. THESE ARE JUST PROMPTS THAT MAY NOT BE RELEVANT AND YOU CAN PUT MORE DETAILED EXPLAINATIONS IN YOUR NOTE SECTIONS INSTEAD.

NAME OF ALTER: _____

AGE: _____

BIRTHDAY: _____

GENDER IDENTITY: _____

SEXUALITY PREFERENCE (E.G. LGBTQ STRAIGHT ETC):
_____

LIKES:
_____
_____
_____
_____

DISLIKES:
_____
_____
_____
_____

RELEVANT CATEGORIZATIONS

HOST/ANP   INTERNAL HELPER   TEEN ALTER   OPPOSITE SEX ALTER   LITTLE
INTROJECT   PROTECTOR   EMOTIONAL   FRAGMENT   LOCKED   PERSECUTOR
OTHER_____

NOTES: _____
_____
_____
_____
_____
_____
_____

MEMBERS INTRODUCTION & PROFILE

USE THESE PROFILES TO INTRODUCE YOURSELF AND FOR OTHER NEW ALTERS TO USE TO INTRODUCE THEMSELVES TO THE REST OF YOUR SYSTEM AND LEARN MORE ABOUT THEM. THESE ARE JUST PROMPTS THAT MAY NOT BE RELEVANT AND YOU CAN PUT MORE DETAILED EXPLAINATIONS IN YOUR NOTE SECTIONS INSTEAD.

NAME OF ALTER: _____

AGE: _____

BIRTHDAY: _____

GENDER IDENTITY: _____

SEXUALITY PREFERENCE (E.G. LGBTQ STRAIGHT ETC): _____

LIKES:
_____
_____
_____
_____

DISLIKES:
_____
_____
_____
_____

RELEVANT CATEGORIZATIONS

| HOST/ANP | INTERNAL HELPER | TEEN ALTER | OPPOSITE SEX ALTER | LITTLE |
| INTROJECT | PROTECTOR | EMOTIONAL | FRAGMENT | LOCKED | PERSECUTOR |

OTHER _____

NOTES: _____
_____
_____
_____
_____
_____
_____

MEMBERS INTRODUCTION & PROFILE

USE THESE PROFILES TO INTRODUCE YOURSELF AND FOR OTHER NEW ALTERS TO USE TO INTRODUCE THEMSELVES TO THE REST OF YOUR SYSTEM AND LEARN MORE ABOUT THEM. THESE ARE JUST PROMPTS THAT MAY NOT BE RELEVANT AND YOU CAN PUT MORE DETAILED EXPLAINATIONS IN YOUR NOTE SECTIONS INSTEAD.

NAME OF ALTER: _____

AGE: _____

BIRTHDAY: _____

GENDER IDENTITY: _____

SEXUALITY PREFERENCE (E.G. LGBTQ STRAIGHT ETC): _____

LIKES:
_____
_____
_____
_____

DISLIKES:
_____
_____
_____
_____

RELEVANT CATEGORIZATIONS

| HOST/ANP | INTERNAL HELPER | TEEN ALTER | OPPOSITE SEX ALTER | LITTLE |
| INTROJECT | PROTECTOR | EMOTIONAL | FRAGMENT | LOCKED | PERSECUTOR |

OTHER _____

NOTES: _____
_____
_____
_____
_____
_____
_____
_____

MEMBERS INTRODUCTION & PROFILE

USE THESE PROFILES TO INTRODUCE YOURSELF AND FOR OTHER NEW ALTERS TO USE TO INTRODUCE THEMSELVES TO THE REST OF YOUR SYSTEM AND LEARN MORE ABOUT THEM. THESE ARE JUST PROMPTS THAT MAY NOT BE RELEVANT AND YOU CAN PUT MORE DETAILED EXPLAINATIONS IN YOUR NOTE SECTIONS INSTEAD.

NAME OF ALTER: _____

AGE: _____

BIRTHDAY: _____

GENDER IDENTITY: _____

SEXUALITY PREFERENCE (E.G. LGBTQ STRAIGHT ETC): _____

LIKES:
_____
_____
_____
_____

DISLIKES:
_____
_____
_____
_____

RELEVANT CATEGORIZATIONS

| HOST/ANP | INTERNAL HELPER | TEEN ALTER | OPPOSITE SEX ALTER | LITTLE |
| INTROJECT | PROTECTOR | EMOTIONAL | FRAGMENT | LOCKED | PERSECUTOR |

OTHER_____

NOTES: _____
_____
_____
_____
_____
_____
_____
_____

MEMBERS INTRODUCTION & PROFILE

USE THESE PROFILES TO INTRODUCE YOURSELF AND FOR OTHER NEW ALTERS TO USE TO INTRODUCE THEMSELVES TO THE REST OF YOUR SYSTEM AND LEARN MORE ABOUT THEM. THESE ARE JUST PROMPTS THAT MAY NOT BE RELEVANT AND YOU CAN PUT MORE DETAILED EXPLAINATIONS IN YOUR NOTE SECTIONS INSTEAD.

NAME OF ALTER: _____

AGE: _____

BIRTHDAY: _____

GENDER IDENTITY: _____

SEXUALITY PREFERENCE (E.G. LGBTQ STRAIGHT ETC):
_____

LIKES:
_____
_____
_____
_____

DISLIKES:
_____
_____
_____
_____

RELEVANT CATEGORIZATIONS

| HOST/ANP | INTERNAL HELPER | TEEN ALTER | OPPOSITE SEX ALTER | LITTLE |
| INTROJECT | PROTECTOR | EMOTIONAL | FRAGMENT | LOCKED | PERSECUTOR |

OTHER _____

NOTES: _____
_____
_____
_____
_____
_____
_____

MEMBERS INTRODUCTION & PROFILE

USE THESE PROFILES TO INTRODUCE YOURSELF AND FOR OTHER NEW ALTERS TO USE TO INTRODUCE THEMSELVES TO THE REST OF YOUR SYSTEM AND LEARN MORE ABOUT THEM. THESE ARE JUST PROMPTS THAT MAY NOT BE RELEVANT AND YOU CAN PUT MORE DETAILED EXPLAINATIONS IN YOUR NOTE SECTIONS INSTEAD.

NAME OF ALTER: _____

AGE: _____

BIRTHDAY: _____

GENDER IDENTITY: _____

SEXUALITY PREFERENCE (E.G. LGBTQ STRAIGHT ETC): _____

LIKES:
_____
_____
_____
_____

DISLIKES:
_____
_____
_____
_____

RELEVANT CATEGORIZATIONS

| HOST/ANP | INTERNAL HELPER | TEEN ALTER | OPPOSITE SEX ALTER | LITTLE |
| INTROJECT | PROTECTOR | EMOTIONAL | FRAGMENT | LOCKED | PERSECUTOR |

OTHER _____

NOTES:
_____
_____
_____
_____
_____
_____

MEMBERS INTRODUCTION & PROFILE

USE THESE PROFILES TO INTRODUCE YOURSELF AND FOR OTHER NEW ALTERS TO USE TO INTRODUCE THEMSELVES TO THE REST OF YOUR SYSTEM AND LEARN MORE ABOUT THEM. THESE ARE JUST PROMPTS THAT MAY NOT BE RELEVANT AND YOU CAN PUT MORE DETAILED EXPLAINATIONS IN YOUR NOTE SECTIONS INSTEAD.

NAME OF ALTER: _____

AGE: _____

BIRTHDAY: _____

GENDER IDENTITY: _____

SEXUALITY PREFERENCE (E.G. LGBTQ STRAIGHT ETC):
_____

LIKES:
_____
_____
_____
_____

DISLIKES:
_____
_____
_____
_____

RELEVANT CATEGORIZATIONS

| HOST/ANP | INTERNAL HELPER | TEEN ALTER | OPPOSITE SEX ALTER | LITTLE |
| INTROJECT | PROTECTOR | EMOTIONAL | FRAGMENT | LOCKED | PERSECUTOR |

OTHER _____

NOTES: _____
_____
_____
_____
_____
_____
_____

MEMBERS INTRODUCTION & PROFILE

USE THESE PROFILES TO INTRODUCE YOURSELF AND FOR OTHER NEW ALTERS TO USE TO INTRODUCE THEMSELVES TO THE REST OF YOUR SYSTEM AND LEARN MORE ABOUT THEM. THESE ARE JUST PROMPTS THAT MAY NOT BE RELEVANT AND YOU CAN PUT MORE DETAILED EXPLAINATIONS IN YOUR NOTE SECTIONS INSTEAD.

NAME OF ALTER: _____

AGE: _____

BIRTHDAY: _____

GENDER IDENTITY: _____

SEXUALITY PREFERENCE (E.G. LGBTQ STRAIGHT ETC):
_____

LIKES:
_____
_____
_____
_____

DISLIKES:
_____
_____
_____
_____

RELEVANT CATEGORIZATIONS

| HOST/ANP | INTERNAL HELPER | TEEN ALTER | OPPOSITE SEX ALTER | LITTLE |
| INTROJECT | PROTECTOR | EMOTIONAL | FRAGMENT | LOCKED | PERSECUTOR |

OTHER _____

NOTES:
_____
_____
_____
_____
_____
_____
_____
_____

MEMBERS INTRODUCTION & PROFILE

USE THESE PROFILES TO INTRODUCE YOURSELF AND FOR OTHER NEW ALTERS TO USE TO INTRODUCE THEMSELVES TO THE REST OF YOUR SYSTEM AND LEARN MORE ABOUT THEM. THESE ARE JUST PROMPTS THAT MAY NOT BE RELEVANT AND YOU CAN PUT MORE DETAILED EXPLAINATIONS IN YOUR NOTE SECTIONS INSTEAD.

NAME OF ALTER: _____

AGE: _____

BIRTHDAY: _____

GENDER IDENTITY: _____

SEXUALITY PREFERENCE (E.G. LGBTQ STRAIGHT ETC):
_____

LIKES:
_____
_____
_____
_____

DISLIKES:
_____
_____
_____
_____

RELEVANT CATEGORIZATIONS

HOST/ANP   INTERNAL HELPER   TEEN ALTER   OPPOSITE SEX ALTER   LITTLE
INTROJECT   PROTECTOR   EMOTIONAL   FRAGMENT   LOCKED   PERSECUTOR
OTHER_____

NOTES: _____
_____
_____
_____
_____
_____
_____

MEMBERS INTRODUCTION & PROFILE

USE THESE PROFILES TO INTRODUCE YOURSELF AND FOR OTHER NEW ALTERS TO USE TO INTRODUCE THEMSELVES TO THE REST OF YOUR SYSTEM AND LEARN MORE ABOUT THEM. THESE ARE JUST PROMPTS THAT MAY NOT BE RELEVANT AND YOU CAN PUT MORE DETAILED EXPLAINATIONS IN YOUR NOTE SECTIONS INSTEAD.

NAME OF ALTER: _____

AGE: _____

BIRTHDAY: _____

GENDER IDENTITY: _____

SEXUALITY PREFERENCE (E.G. LGBTQ STRAIGHT ETC):
_____

LIKES:
_____
_____
_____
_____

DISLIKES:
_____
_____
_____
_____

RELEVANT CATEGORIZATIONS

HOST/ANP   INTERNAL HELPER   TEEN ALTER   OPPOSITE SEX ALTER   LITTLE
INTROJECT   PROTECTOR   EMOTIONAL   FRAGMENT   LOCKED   PERSECUTOR
OTHER _____

NOTES: _____
_____
_____
_____
_____
_____
_____

MEMBERS INTRODUCTION & PROFILE

USE THESE PROFILES TO INTRODUCE YOURSELF AND FOR OTHER NEW ALTERS TO USE TO INTRODUCE THEMSELVES TO THE REST OF YOUR SYSTEM AND LEARN MORE ABOUT THEM. THESE ARE JUST PROMPTS THAT MAY NOT BE RELEVANT AND YOU CAN PUT MORE DETAILED EXPLAINATIONS IN YOUR NOTE SECTIONS INSTEAD.

NAME OF ALTER: _____

AGE: _____

BIRTHDAY: _____

GENDER IDENTITY: _____

SEXUALITY PREFERENCE (E.G. LGBTQ STRAIGHT ETC): _____

LIKES:
_____
_____
_____
_____

DISLIKES:
_____
_____
_____
_____

RELEVANT CATEGORIZATIONS

| HOST/ANP | INTERNAL HELPER | TEEN ALTER | OPPOSITE SEX ALTER | LITTLE |
| INTROJECT | PROTECTOR | EMOTIONAL | FRAGMENT | LOCKED | PERSECUTOR |

OTHER _____

NOTES: _____
_____
_____
_____
_____
_____
_____

MEMBERS INTRODUCTION & PROFILE

USE THESE PROFILES TO INTRODUCE YOURSELF AND FOR OTHER NEW ALTERS TO USE TO INTRODUCE THEMSELVES TO THE REST OF YOUR SYSTEM AND LEARN MORE ABOUT THEM. THESE ARE JUST PROMPTS THAT MAY NOT BE RELEVANT AND YOU CAN PUT MORE DETAILED EXPLAINATIONS IN YOUR NOTE SECTIONS INSTEAD.

NAME OF ALTER: _____

AGE: _____

BIRTHDAY: _____

GENDER IDENTITY: _____

SEXUALITY PREFERENCE (E.G. LGBTQ STRAIGHT ETC):
_____

LIKES:
_____
_____
_____
_____

DISLIKES:
_____
_____
_____
_____

RELEVANT CATEGORIZATIONS

| HOST/ANP | INTERNAL HELPER | TEEN ALTER | OPPOSITE SEX ALTER | LITTLE |
| INTROJECT | PROTECTOR | EMOTIONAL | FRAGMENT | LOCKED | PERSECUTOR |

OTHER _____

NOTES: _____
_____
_____
_____
_____
_____
_____

MEMBERS INTRODUCTION & PROFILE

USE THESE PROFILES TO INTRODUCE YOURSELF AND FOR OTHER NEW ALTERS TO USE TO INTRODUCE THEMSELVES TO THE REST OF YOUR SYSTEM AND LEARN MORE ABOUT THEM. THESE ARE JUST PROMPTS THAT MAY NOT BE RELEVANT AND YOU CAN PUT MORE DETAILED EXPLAINATIONS IN YOUR NOTE SECTIONS INSTEAD.

NAME OF ALTER: _____

AGE: _____

BIRTHDAY: _____

GENDER IDENTITY: _____

SEXUALITY PREFERENCE (E.G. LGBTQ STRAIGHT ETC): _____

LIKES:
_____
_____
_____
_____

DISLIKES:
_____
_____
_____
_____

RELEVANT CATEGORIZATIONS

HOST/ANP   INTERNAL HELPER   TEEN ALTER   OPPOSITE SEX ALTER   LITTLE
INTROJECT   PROTECTOR   EMOTIONAL   FRAGMENT   LOCKED   PERSECUTOR
OTHER _____

NOTES: _____
_____
_____
_____
_____
_____
_____

MEMBERS INTRODUCTION & PROFILE

USE THESE PROFILES TO INTRODUCE YOURSELF AND FOR OTHER NEW ALTERS TO USE TO INTRODUCE THEMSELVES TO THE REST OF YOUR SYSTEM AND LEARN MORE ABOUT THEM. THESE ARE JUST PROMPTS THAT MAY NOT BE RELEVANT AND YOU CAN PUT MORE DETAILED EXPLAINATIONS IN YOUR NOTE SECTIONS INSTEAD.

NAME OF ALTER: _____

AGE: _____

BIRTHDAY: _____

GENDER IDENTITY: _____

SEXUALITY PREFERENCE (E.G. LGBTQ STRAIGHT ETC):
_____

LIKES:
_____
_____
_____
_____

DISLIKES:
_____
_____
_____
_____

RELEVANT CATEGORIZATIONS

HOST/ANP   INTERNAL HELPER   TEEN ALTER   OPPOSITE SEX ALTER   LITTLE
INTROJECT   PROTECTOR   EMOTIONAL   FRAGMENT   LOCKED   PERSECUTOR
OTHER_____

NOTES: _____
_____
_____
_____
_____
_____
_____

MEMBERS INTRODUCTION & PROFILE

USE THESE PROFILES TO INTRODUCE YOURSELF AND FOR OTHER NEW ALTERS TO USE TO INTRODUCE THEMSELVES TO THE REST OF YOUR SYSTEM AND LEARN MORE ABOUT THEM. THESE ARE JUST PROMPTS THAT MAY NOT BE RELEVANT AND YOU CAN PUT MORE DETAILED EXPLAINATIONS IN YOUR NOTE SECTIONS INSTEAD.

NAME OF ALTER: _____

AGE: _____

BIRTHDAY: _____

GENDER IDENTITY: _____

SEXUALITY PREFERENCE (E.G. LGBTQ STRAIGHT ETC):
_____

LIKES:
_____
_____
_____
_____

DISLIKES:
_____
_____
_____
_____

RELEVANT CATEGORIZATIONS

| HOST/ANP | INTERNAL HELPER | TEEN ALTER | OPPOSITE SEX ALTER | LITTLE |
| INTROJECT | PROTECTOR | EMOTIONAL | FRAGMENT | LOCKED | PERSECUTOR |

OTHER_____

NOTES: _____
_____
_____
_____
_____
_____
_____
_____

MEMBERS INTRODUCTION & PROFILE

USE THESE PROFILES TO INTRODUCE YOURSELF AND FOR OTHER NEW ALTERS TO USE TO INTRODUCE THEMSELVES TO THE REST OF YOUR SYSTEM AND LEARN MORE ABOUT THEM. THESE ARE JUST PROMPTS THAT MAY NOT BE RELEVANT AND YOU CAN PUT MORE DETAILED EXPLAINATIONS IN YOUR NOTE SECTIONS INSTEAD.

NAME OF ALTER: _____

AGE: _____

BIRTHDAY: _____

GENDER IDENTITY: _____

SEXUALITY PREFERENCE (E.G. LGBTQ STRAIGHT ETC):
_____

LIKES:
_____
_____
_____
_____

DISLIKES:
_____
_____
_____
_____

RELEVANT CATEGORIZATIONS

| HOST/ANP | INTERNAL HELPER | TEEN ALTER | OPPOSITE SEX ALTER | LITTLE |
| INTROJECT | PROTECTOR | EMOTIONAL | FRAGMENT | LOCKED | PERSECUTOR |

OTHER _____

NOTES: _____
_____
_____
_____
_____
_____
_____

MEMBERS INTRODUCTION & PROFILE

USE THESE PROFILES TO INTRODUCE YOURSELF AND FOR OTHER NEW ALTERS TO USE TO INTRODUCE THEMSELVES TO THE REST OF YOUR SYSTEM AND LEARN MORE ABOUT THEM. THESE ARE JUST PROMPTS THAT MAY NOT BE RELEVANT AND YOU CAN PUT MORE DETAILED EXPLAINATIONS IN YOUR NOTE SECTIONS INSTEAD.

NAME OF ALTER: _____

AGE: _____

BIRTHDAY: _____

GENDER IDENTITY: _____

SEXUALITY PREFERENCE (E.G. LGBTQ STRAIGHT ETC):
_____

LIKES:
_____
_____
_____
_____

DISLIKES:
_____
_____
_____
_____

RELEVANT CATEGORIZATIONS

HOST/ANP   INTERNAL HELPER   TEEN ALTER   OPPOSITE SEX ALTER   LITTLE
INTROJECT   PROTECTOR   EMOTIONAL   FRAGMENT   LOCKED   PERSECUTOR
OTHER _____

NOTES: _____
_____
_____
_____
_____
_____

MEMBERS INTRODUCTION & PROFILE

USE THESE PROFILES TO INTRODUCE YOURSELF AND FOR OTHER NEW ALTERS TO USE TO INTRODUCE THEMSELVES TO THE REST OF YOUR SYSTEM AND LEARN MORE ABOUT THEM. THESE ARE JUST PROMPTS THAT MAY NOT BE RELEVANT AND YOU CAN PUT MORE DETAILED EXPLAINATIONS IN YOUR NOTE SECTIONS INSTEAD.

NAME OF ALTER: _____

AGE: _____

BIRTHDAY: _____

GENDER IDENTITY: _____

SEXUALITY PREFERENCE (E.G. LGBTQ STRAIGHT ETC):
_____

LIKES:
_____
_____
_____
_____

DISLIKES:
_____
_____
_____
_____

RELEVANT CATEGORIZATIONS

HOST/ANP   INTERNAL HELPER   TEEN ALTER   OPPOSITE SEX ALTER   LITTLE
INTROJECT   PROTECTOR   EMOTIONAL   FRAGMENT   LOCKED   PERSECUTOR
OTHER _____

NOTES: _____
_____
_____
_____
_____
_____
_____

MEMBERS INTRODUCTION & PROFILE

USE THESE PROFILES TO INTRODUCE YOURSELF AND FOR OTHER NEW ALTERS TO USE TO INTRODUCE THEMSELVES TO THE REST OF YOUR SYSTEM AND LEARN MORE ABOUT THEM. THESE ARE JUST PROMPTS THAT MAY NOT BE RELEVANT AND YOU CAN PUT MORE DETAILED EXPLAINATIONS IN YOUR NOTE SECTIONS INSTEAD.

NAME OF ALTER: _____

AGE: _____

BIRTHDAY: _____

GENDER IDENTITY: _____

SEXUALITY PREFERENCE (E.G. LGBTQ STRAIGHT ETC):
_____

LIKES:
_____
_____
_____
_____

DISLIKES:
_____
_____
_____
_____

RELEVANT CATEGORIZATIONS

| HOST/ANP | INTERNAL HELPER | TEEN ALTER | OPPOSITE SEX ALTER | LITTLE |
| INTROJECT | PROTECTOR | EMOTIONAL | FRAGMENT | LOCKED | PERSECUTOR |

OTHER _____

NOTES: _____
_____
_____
_____
_____
_____
_____

MEMBERS INTRODUCTION & PROFILE

USE THESE PROFILES TO INTRODUCE YOURSELF AND FOR OTHER NEW ALTERS TO USE TO INTRODUCE THEMSELVES TO THE REST OF YOUR SYSTEM AND LEARN MORE ABOUT THEM. THESE ARE JUST PROMPTS THAT MAY NOT BE RELEVANT AND YOU CAN PUT MORE DETAILED EXPLAINATIONS IN YOUR NOTE SECTIONS INSTEAD.

NAME OF ALTER: _____

AGE: _____

BIRTHDAY: _____

GENDER IDENTITY: _____

SEXUALITY PREFERENCE (E.G. LGBTQ STRAIGHT ETC):
_____

LIKES:
_____
_____
_____
_____

DISLIKES:
_____
_____
_____
_____

RELEVANT CATEGORIZATIONS

HOST/ANP   INTERNAL HELPER   TEEN ALTER   OPPOSITE SEX ALTER   LITTLE   INTROJECT   PROTECTOR   EMOTIONAL   FRAGMENT   LOCKED   PERSECUTOR

OTHER _____

NOTES: _____
_____
_____
_____
_____
_____
_____
_____

MEMBERS INTRODUCTION & PROFILE

USE THESE PROFILES TO INTRODUCE YOURSELF AND FOR OTHER NEW ALTERS TO USE TO INTRODUCE THEMSELVES TO THE REST OF YOUR SYSTEM AND LEARN MORE ABOUT THEM. THESE ARE JUST PROMPTS THAT MAY NOT BE RELEVANT AND YOU CAN PUT MORE DETAILED EXPLAINATIONS IN YOUR NOTE SECTIONS INSTEAD.

NAME OF ALTER: _____

AGE: _____

BIRTHDAY: _____

GENDER IDENTITY: _____

SEXUALITY PREFERENCE (E.G. LGBTQ STRAIGHT ETC):
_____

LIKES:
_____
_____
_____
_____

DISLIKES:
_____
_____
_____
_____

RELEVANT CATEGORIZATIONS

HOST/ANP   INTERNAL HELPER   TEEN ALTER   OPPOSITE SEX ALTER   LITTLE
INTROJECT   PROTECTOR   EMOTIONAL   FRAGMENT   LOCKED   PERSECUTOR
OTHER_____

NOTES: _____
_____
_____
_____
_____
_____
_____

MEMBERS INTRODUCTION & PROFILE

USE THESE PROFILES TO INTRODUCE YOURSELF AND FOR OTHER NEW ALTERS TO USE TO INTRODUCE THEMSELVES TO THE REST OF YOUR SYSTEM AND LEARN MORE ABOUT THEM. THESE ARE JUST PROMPTS THAT MAY NOT BE RELEVANT AND YOU CAN PUT MORE DETAILED EXPLAINATIONS IN YOUR NOTE SECTIONS INSTEAD.

NAME OF ALTER: _____

AGE: _____

BIRTHDAY: _____

GENDER IDENTITY: _____

SEXUALITY PREFERENCE (E.G. LGBTQ STRAIGHT ETC):
_____

LIKES:
_____
_____
_____
_____

DISLIKES:
_____
_____
_____
_____

RELEVANT CATEGORIZATIONS

HOST/ANP   INTERNAL HELPER   TEEN ALTER   OPPOSITE SEX ALTER   LITTLE
INTROJECT   PROTECTOR   EMOTIONAL   FRAGMENT   LOCKED   PERSECUTOR
OTHER_____

NOTES: _____
_____
_____
_____
_____
_____
_____

MEMBERS INTRODUCTION & PROFILE

USE THESE PROFILES TO INTRODUCE YOURSELF AND FOR OTHER NEW ALTERS TO USE TO INTRODUCE THEMSELVES TO THE REST OF YOUR SYSTEM AND LEARN MORE ABOUT THEM. THESE ARE JUST PROMPTS THAT MAY NOT BE RELEVANT AND YOU CAN PUT MORE DETAILED EXPLAINATIONS IN YOUR NOTE SECTIONS INSTEAD.

NAME OF ALTER: _____

AGE: _____

BIRTHDAY: _____

GENDER IDENTITY: _____

SEXUALITY PREFERENCE (E.G. LGBTQ STRAIGHT ETC):
_____

LIKES:
_____
_____
_____
_____

DISLIKES:
_____
_____
_____
_____

RELEVANT CATEGORIZATIONS

HOST/ANP   INTERNAL HELPER   TEEN ALTER   OPPOSITE SEX ALTER   LITTLE
INTROJECT   PROTECTOR   EMOTIONAL   FRAGMENT   LOCKED   PERSECUTOR
OTHER_____

NOTES: _____
_____
_____
_____
_____
_____
_____

MEMBERS INTRODUCTION & PROFILE

USE THESE PROFILES TO INTRODUCE YOURSELF AND FOR OTHER NEW ALTERS TO USE TO INTRODUCE THEMSELVES TO THE REST OF YOUR SYSTEM AND LEARN MORE ABOUT THEM. THESE ARE JUST PROMPTS THAT MAY NOT BE RELEVANT AND YOU CAN PUT MORE DETAILED EXPLAINATIONS IN YOUR NOTE SECTIONS INSTEAD.

NAME OF ALTER: _____

AGE: _____

BIRTHDAY: _____

GENDER IDENTITY: _____

SEXUALITY PREFERENCE (E.G. LGBTQ STRAIGHT ETC): _____

LIKES:
_____
_____
_____
_____

DISLIKES:
_____
_____
_____
_____

RELEVANT CATEGORIZATIONS

HOST/ANP   INTERNAL HELPER   TEEN ALTER   OPPOSITE SEX ALTER   LITTLE
INTROJECT   PROTECTOR   EMOTIONAL   FRAGMENT   LOCKED   PERSECUTOR
OTHER_____

NOTES: _____
_____
_____
_____
_____
_____
_____

MEMBERS INTRODUCTION & PROFILE

USE THESE PROFILES TO INTRODUCE YOURSELF AND FOR OTHER NEW ALTERS TO USE TO INTRODUCE THEMSELVES TO THE REST OF YOUR SYSTEM AND LEARN MORE ABOUT THEM. THESE ARE JUST PROMPTS THAT MAY NOT BE RELEVANT AND YOU CAN PUT MORE DETAILED EXPLAINATIONS IN YOUR NOTE SECTIONS INSTEAD.

NAME OF ALTER: _____

AGE: _____

BIRTHDAY: _____

GENDER IDENTITY: _____

SEXUALITY PREFERENCE (E.G. LGBTQ STRAIGHT ETC):
_____

LIKES:
_____
_____
_____
_____

DISLIKES:
_____
_____
_____
_____

RELEVANT CATEGORIZATIONS

HOST/ANP   INTERNAL HELPER   TEEN ALTER   OPPOSITE SEX ALTER   LITTLE   INTROJECT   PROTECTOR   EMOTIONAL   FRAGMENT   LOCKED   PERSECUTOR
OTHER_____

NOTES: _____
_____
_____
_____
_____
_____
_____

MEMBERS INTRODUCTION & PROFILE

USE THESE PROFILES TO INTRODUCE YOURSELF AND FOR OTHER NEW ALTERS TO USE TO INTRODUCE THEMSELVES TO THE REST OF YOUR SYSTEM AND LEARN MORE ABOUT THEM. THESE ARE JUST PROMPTS THAT MAY NOT BE RELEVANT AND YOU CAN PUT MORE DETAILED EXPLAINATIONS IN YOUR NOTE SECTIONS INSTEAD.

NAME OF ALTER: _____

AGE: _____

BIRTHDAY: _____

GENDER IDENTITY: _____

SEXUALITY PREFERENCE (E.G. LGBTQ STRAIGHT ETC):
_____

LIKES:
_____
_____
_____
_____

DISLIKES:
_____
_____
_____
_____

RELEVANT CATEGORIZATIONS

HOST/ANP   INTERNAL HELPER   TEEN ALTER   OPPOSITE SEX ALTER   LITTLE
INTROJECT   PROTECTOR   EMOTIONAL   FRAGMENT   LOCKED   PERSECUTOR
OTHER _____

NOTES: _____
_____
_____
_____
_____
_____
_____

MEMBERS INTRODUCTION & PROFILE

USE THESE PROFILES TO INTRODUCE YOURSELF AND FOR OTHER NEW ALTERS TO USE TO INTRODUCE THEMSELVES TO THE REST OF YOUR SYSTEM AND LEARN MORE ABOUT THEM. THESE ARE JUST PROMPTS THAT MAY NOT BE RELEVANT AND YOU CAN PUT MORE DETAILED EXPLAINATIONS IN YOUR NOTE SECTIONS INSTEAD.

NAME OF ALTER: _____

AGE: _____

BIRTHDAY: _____

GENDER IDENTITY: _____

SEXUALITY PREFERENCE (E.G. LGBTQ STRAIGHT ETC):
_____

LIKES:
_____
_____
_____
_____

DISLIKES:
_____
_____
_____
_____

RELEVANT CATEGORIZATIONS

| HOST/ANP | INTERNAL HELPER | TEEN ALTER | OPPOSITE SEX ALTER | LITTLE |
| INTROJECT | PROTECTOR | EMOTIONAL | FRAGMENT | LOCKED | PERSECUTOR |

OTHER _____

NOTES: _____
_____
_____
_____
_____
_____
_____
_____

MEMBERS INTRODUCTION & PROFILE

USE THESE PROFILES TO INTRODUCE YOURSELF AND FOR OTHER NEW ALTERS TO USE TO INTRODUCE THEMSELVES TO THE REST OF YOUR SYSTEM AND LEARN MORE ABOUT THEM. THESE ARE JUST PROMPTS THAT MAY NOT BE RELEVANT AND YOU CAN PUT MORE DETAILED EXPLAINATIONS IN YOUR NOTE SECTIONS INSTEAD.

NAME OF ALTER: _____

AGE: _____

BIRTHDAY: _____

GENDER IDENTITY: _____

SEXUALITY PREFERENCE (E.G. LGBTQ STRAIGHT ETC):
_____

LIKES:
_____
_____
_____
_____

DISLIKES:
_____
_____
_____
_____

RELEVANT CATEGORIZATIONS

HOST/ANP   INTERNAL HELPER   TEEN ALTER   OPPOSITE SEX ALTER   LITTLE
INTROJECT   PROTECTOR   EMOTIONAL   FRAGMENT   LOCKED   PERSECUTOR
OTHER _____

NOTES: _____
_____
_____
_____
_____
_____
_____

MEMBERS INTRODUCTION & PROFILE

USE THESE PROFILES TO INTRODUCE YOURSELF AND FOR OTHER NEW ALTERS TO USE TO INTRODUCE THEMSELVES TO THE REST OF YOUR SYSTEM AND LEARN MORE ABOUT THEM. THESE ARE JUST PROMPTS THAT MAY NOT BE RELEVANT AND YOU CAN PUT MORE DETAILED EXPLAINATIONS IN YOUR NOTE SECTIONS INSTEAD.

NAME OF ALTER: _____

AGE: _____

BIRTHDAY: _____

GENDER IDENTITY: _____

SEXUALITY PREFERENCE (E.G. LGBTQ STRAIGHT ETC):
_____

LIKES:
_____
_____
_____
_____

DISLIKES:
_____
_____
_____
_____

RELEVANT CATEGORIZATIONS

| HOST/ANP | INTERNAL HELPER | TEEN ALTER | OPPOSITE SEX ALTER | LITTLE |
| INTROJECT | PROTECTOR | EMOTIONAL | FRAGMENT | LOCKED | PERSECUTOR |

OTHER _____

NOTES: _____
_____
_____
_____
_____
_____
_____

MEMBERS INTRODUCTION & PROFILE

USE THESE PROFILES TO INTRODUCE YOURSELF AND FOR OTHER NEW ALTERS TO USE TO INTRODUCE THEMSELVES TO THE REST OF YOUR SYSTEM AND LEARN MORE ABOUT THEM. THESE ARE JUST PROMPTS THAT MAY NOT BE RELEVANT AND YOU CAN PUT MORE DETAILED EXPLAINATIONS IN YOUR NOTE SECTIONS INSTEAD.

NAME OF ALTER: _____

AGE: _____

BIRTHDAY: _____

GENDER IDENTITY: _____

SEXUALITY PREFERENCE (E.G. LGBTQ STRAIGHT ETC): _____

LIKES:
_____
_____
_____
_____

DISLIKES:
_____
_____
_____
_____

RELEVANT CATEGORIZATIONS

HOST/ANP   INTERNAL HELPER   TEEN ALTER   OPPOSITE SEX ALTER   LITTLE
INTROJECT   PROTECTOR   EMOTIONAL   FRAGMENT   LOCKED   PERSECUTOR
OTHER _____

NOTES: _____
_____
_____
_____
_____
_____
_____

MEMBERS INTRODUCTION & PROFILE

USE THESE PROFILES TO INTRODUCE YOURSELF AND FOR OTHER NEW ALTERS TO USE TO INTRODUCE THEMSELVES TO THE REST OF YOUR SYSTEM AND LEARN MORE ABOUT THEM. THESE ARE JUST PROMPTS THAT MAY NOT BE RELEVANT AND YOU CAN PUT MORE DETAILED EXPLAINATIONS IN YOUR NOTE SECTIONS INSTEAD.

NAME OF ALTER: _____

AGE: _____

BIRTHDAY: _____

GENDER IDENTITY: _____

SEXUALITY PREFERENCE (E.G. LGBTQ STRAIGHT ETC): _____

LIKES:
_____
_____
_____
_____

DISLIKES:
_____
_____
_____
_____

RELEVANT CATEGORIZATIONS

HOST/ANP   INTERNAL HELPER   TEEN ALTER   OPPOSITE SEX ALTER   LITTLE   INTROJECT   PROTECTOR   EMOTIONAL   FRAGMENT   LOCKED   PERSECUTOR   OTHER _____

NOTES: _____
_____
_____
_____
_____
_____
_____

MEMBERS INTRODUCTION & PROFILE

USE THESE PROFILES TO INTRODUCE YOURSELF AND FOR OTHER NEW ALTERS TO USE TO INTRODUCE THEMSELVES TO THE REST OF YOUR SYSTEM AND LEARN MORE ABOUT THEM. THESE ARE JUST PROMPTS THAT MAY NOT BE RELEVANT AND YOU CAN PUT MORE DETAILED EXPLAINATIONS IN YOUR NOTE SECTIONS INSTEAD.

NAME OF ALTER: _____

AGE: _____

BIRTHDAY: _____

GENDER IDENTITY: _____

SEXUALITY PREFERENCE (E.G. LGBTQ STRAIGHT ETC):
_____

LIKES:
_____
_____
_____
_____

DISLIKES:
_____
_____
_____
_____

RELEVANT CATEGORIZATIONS

HOST/ANP   INTERNAL HELPER   TEEN ALTER   OPPOSITE SEX ALTER   LITTLE   INTROJECT   PROTECTOR   EMOTIONAL   FRAGMENT   LOCKED   PERSECUTOR

OTHER _____

NOTES: _____
_____
_____
_____
_____
_____
_____

MEMBERS INTRODUCTION & PROFILE

USE THESE PROFILES TO INTRODUCE YOURSELF AND FOR OTHER NEW ALTERS TO USE TO INTRODUCE THEMSELVES TO THE REST OF YOUR SYSTEM AND LEARN MORE ABOUT THEM. THESE ARE JUST PROMPTS THAT MAY NOT BE RELEVANT AND YOU CAN PUT MORE DETAILED EXPLAINATIONS IN YOUR NOTE SECTIONS INSTEAD.

NAME OF ALTER: _____

AGE: _____

BIRTHDAY: _____

GENDER IDENTITY: _____

SEXUALITY PREFERENCE (E.G. LGBTQ STRAIGHT ETC):
_____

LIKES:
_____
_____
_____
_____

DISLIKES:
_____
_____
_____
_____

RELEVANT CATEGORIZATIONS

HOST/ANP   INTERNAL HELPER   TEEN ALTER   OPPOSITE SEX ALTER   LITTLE
INTROJECT   PROTECTOR   EMOTIONAL   FRAGMENT   LOCKED   PERSECUTOR
OTHER_____

NOTES: _____
_____
_____
_____
_____
_____
_____

MEMBERS INTRODUCTION & PROFILE

USE THESE PROFILES TO INTRODUCE YOURSELF AND FOR OTHER NEW ALTERS TO USE TO INTRODUCE THEMSELVES TO THE REST OF YOUR SYSTEM AND LEARN MORE ABOUT THEM. THESE ARE JUST PROMPTS THAT MAY NOT BE RELEVANT AND YOU CAN PUT MORE DETAILED EXPLAINATIONS IN YOUR NOTE SECTIONS INSTEAD.

NAME OF ALTER: _____

AGE: _____

BIRTHDAY: _____

GENDER IDENTITY: _____

SEXUALITY PREFERENCE (E.G. LGBTQ STRAIGHT ETC): _____

LIKES:
_____
_____
_____
_____

DISLIKES:
_____
_____
_____
_____

RELEVANT CATEGORIZATIONS

HOST/ANP   INTERNAL HELPER   TEEN ALTER   OPPOSITE SEX ALTER   LITTLE
INTROJECT   PROTECTOR   EMOTIONAL   FRAGMENT   LOCKED   PERSECUTOR
OTHER_____

NOTES: _____
_____
_____
_____
_____
_____
_____
_____

MEMBERS INTRODUCTION & PROFILE

USE THESE PROFILES TO INTRODUCE YOURSELF AND FOR OTHER NEW ALTERS TO USE TO INTRODUCE THEMSELVES TO THE REST OF YOUR SYSTEM AND LEARN MORE ABOUT THEM. THESE ARE JUST PROMPTS THAT MAY NOT BE RELEVANT AND YOU CAN PUT MORE DETAILED EXPLAINATIONS IN YOUR NOTE SECTIONS INSTEAD.

NAME OF ALTER: _____

AGE: _____

BIRTHDAY: _____

GENDER IDENTITY: _____

SEXUALITY PREFERENCE (E.G. LGBTQ STRAIGHT ETC): _____

LIKES:
_____
_____
_____
_____

DISLIKES:
_____
_____
_____
_____

RELEVANT CATEGORIZATIONS

| HOST/ANP | INTERNAL HELPER | TEEN ALTER | OPPOSITE SEX ALTER | LITTLE |
| INTROJECT | PROTECTOR | EMOTIONAL | FRAGMENT | LOCKED | PERSECUTOR |

OTHER _____

NOTES:
_____
_____
_____
_____
_____
_____
_____

SYSTEM MAP

HOW TO USE

- THERE ARE LOTS OF BLANK PAGES FOR YOU TO OUTLINE THE SYSTEM MAP AND JOURNAL PAGES TO ADD DETAILS.
- USE IT TO MAP THE HOST, THE ALTERS, GROUP THEM WITH THE THINGS THEY HAVE IN COMMON (A SOCIAL CLIQUE).
- KEEP IN MIND ELEMENTS LIKE HOW MUCH TIME THEY SPEND OCCUPYING THE BODY, WHO IS THE LEADER, WHO IS A HELPER.
- THINK ABOUT WHO DOES THE ALTER SEEK HELP FROM, WHO DO THEY IN TURN HELP THEMSELVES.
- NOTE THE DIFFERENT RELATIONSHIPS BETWEEN THE ALTERS. E.G. WHO ELSE IS THE ALTER AWARE OF, WHO IS THAT ALTER CLOSES TOO AND WHO ARE THEY MOST DISTANT FROM.
- WHAT TYPE OF JOBS AND PERSONALITIES DOES EACH ALTER HAVE.
- YOU CAN CREATE YOUR MAP HOWEVER YOU LIKE BUT THERE ARE SOME TEMPLATE IDEAS ON THE NEXT PAGE TO HELP YOU IF YOU NEED SOME INSPIRATION !

THINGS TO REMEMBER

- REMEMBER TO DATE YOUR MAP TO SEE HOW IT CHANGES OVER TIME.

SYSTEM MAP LAYOUT INSPIRATION

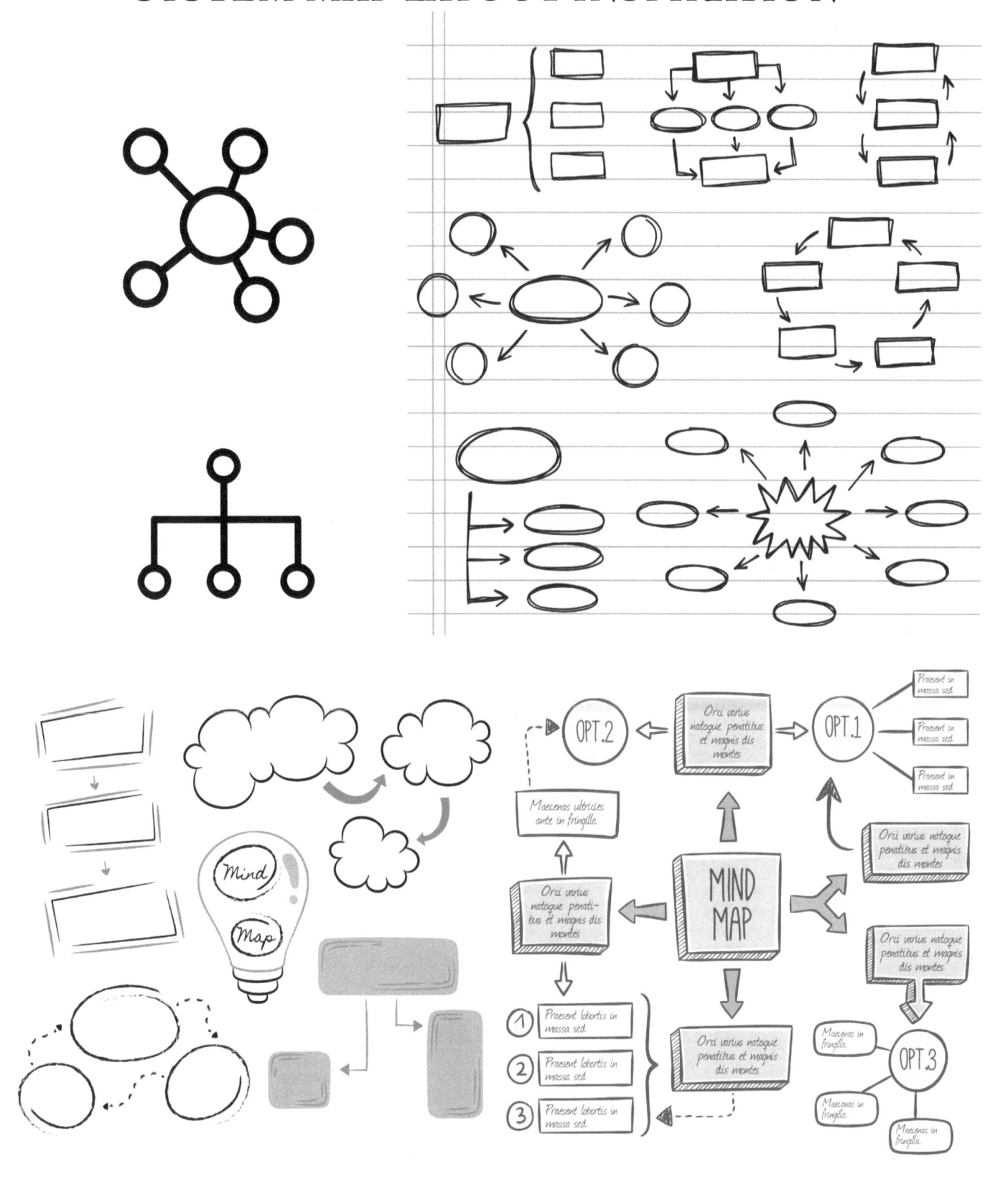

DAILY ENERGY vs MOOD TRACKER

TRACK YOUR DAILY ENERGY AND MOOD USING DIFFERENT COLOURS ON THIS LINE CHART - NOTE YOUR TRIGGERS BELOW.

100

75

50

25

0
ENERGY   MONDAY   TUESDAY   WEDNESDAY   THURSDAY   FRIDAY   SATURDAY   SUNDAY   MOOD

GRATITUDE PROMPTS & QUOTES

There are journal pages next to the prompts so all the alters can answer the prompts to learn more about alters.

GRATITUDE EXERCISE NO.1

WHAT DOES GRATITUDE MEAN?

ANSWER THESE QUESTIONS TO BREAK OUT OF NEGATIVE THOUGHT PATTERNS AND REFOCUS ON THE THINGS THAT MAKE YOU HAPPY AND GRATEFUL.

GRATITUDE EXERCISE NO. 2

WHEN IS GRATITUDE IMPORTANT?

ANSWER THESE QUESTIONS TO BREAK OUT OF NEGATIVE THOUGHT PATTERNS AND REFOCUS ON THE THINGS THAT MAKE YOU HAPPY AND GRATEFUL.

GRATITUDE EXERCISE NO.3

WHO ARE YOU MOST GRATEFUL FOR?

ANSWER THESE QUESTIONS TO BREAK OUT OF NEGATIVE THOUGHT PATTERNS AND REFOCUS ON THE THINGS THAT MAKE YOU HAPPY AND GRATEFUL.

GRATITUDE EXERCISE NO. 4

WHAT MOMENT ARE YOU MOST GRATEFUL FOR?

ANSWER THESE QUESTIONS TO BREAK OUT OF NEGATIVE THOUGHT PATTERNS AND REFOCUS ON THE THINGS THAT MAKE YOU HAPPY AND GRATEFUL.

GRATITUDE EXERCISE NO.5

WHAT BODY PART ARE YOU GRATEFUL FOR?

ANSWER THESE QUESTIONS TO BREAK OUT OF NEGATIVE THOUGHT PATTERNS AND REFOCUS ON THE THINGS THAT MAKE YOU HAPPY AND GRATEFUL.

GRATITUDE EXERCISE NO.6

WHAT HAVE YOU DONE IN YOUR LIFE THAT HAS MADE SOMEONE ELSE HAPPY?

ANSWER THESE QUESTIONS TO BREAK OUT OF NEGATIVE THOUGHT PATTERNS AND REFOCUS ON THE THINGS THAT MAKE YOU HAPPY AND GRATEFUL.

GRATITUDE EXERCISE NO.7

WHAT I HOPE IS YET TO COME...

ANSWER THESE QUESTIONS TO BREAK OUT OF NEGATIVE THOUGHT PATTERNS AND REFOCUS ON THE THINGS THAT MAKE YOU HAPPY AND GRATEFUL.

GRATITUDE EXERCISE NO.8

WHAT IS YOUR THE MOST DELICIOUS FOOD?

ANSWER THESE QUESTIONS TO BREAK OUT OF NEGATIVE THOUGHT PATTERNS AND REFOCUS ON THE THINGS THAT MAKE YOU HAPPY AND GRATEFUL.

GRATITUDE EXERCISE NO.9

WHAT DO YOU LOVE ABOUT YOUR FAVOURITE BOOK

ANSWER THESE QUESTIONS TO BREAK OUT OF NEGATIVE THOUGHT PATTERNS AND REFOCUS ON THE THINGS THAT MAKE YOU HAPPY AND GRATEFUL.

One Minute Meditation

Breathe in through your nose.

Breathe out through your mouth.

Feel air in the depths of your lungs
as you breathe in again.

As you breathe out feel tension
release from your body.

Repeat 3x.

Self Care is not Selfish. It's self respect.

Make Your Head A Nice Place To Live.

honour your needs.

Make Your Head A Nice Place To Live.

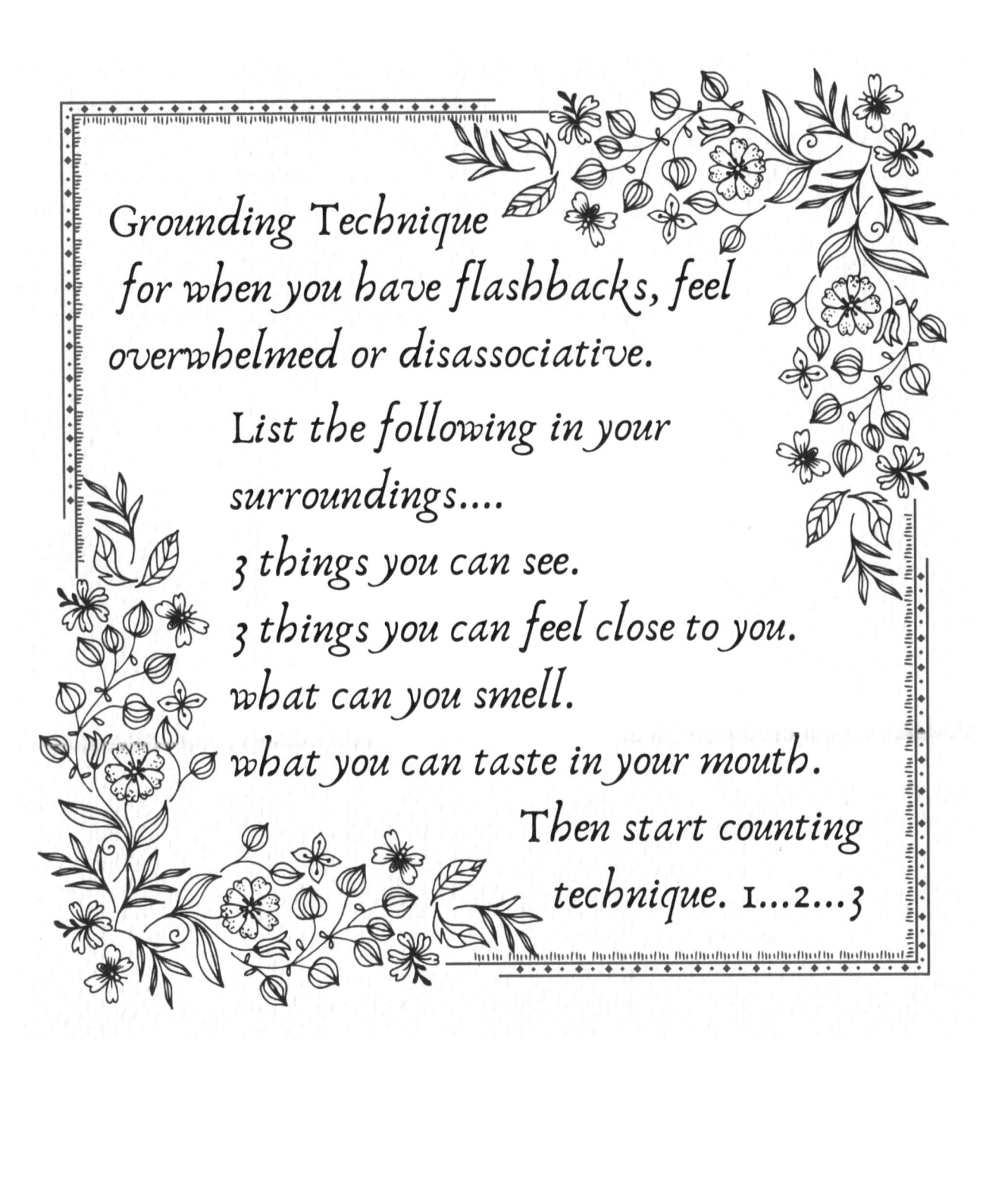

Grounding Technique
for when you have flashbacks, feel overwhelmed or disassociative.

List the following in your surroundings....

3 things you can see.

3 things you can feel close to you.

what can you smell.

what you can taste in your mouth.

Then start counting technique. 1...2...3

"be the things you loved most
about the people who are gone"

DAILY ENERGY vs MOOD TRACKER

TRACK YOUR DAILY ENERGY AND MOOD USING DIFFERENT COLOURS ON THIS LINE CHART - NOTE YOUR TRIGGERS BELOW.

100 ———

75 ——

50 ——

25 ——

0 MONDAY   TUESDAY   WEDNESDAY   THURSDAY   FRIDAY   SATURDAY   SUNDAY

ENERGY   MOOD

DID MENTAL HEALTH AND SYMPTOM CHECK LIST   NAME_____ DATE____

	FREQ. / SEVERITY Y/N	MON	TUES	WED	THURS	FRI	SAT	SUN
OVERALL MOOD	0-5							
ENERGY LEVELS	0-5							
ANXIETY	0-5							
AMNESIA / MEMORY PROBLEMS	Y/N							
RANDOM SWITCH	Y/N							
TRIGGERED SWITCH	Y/N							
DEPRESSION	0-5							
LOTS OF SWITCHING	Y/N							
"EMOTIONAL HANGOVER"	Y/N							
RAPID CYCLING MOOD SWINGS	Y/N							
FEELING OVERWHELMED	0-5							
FEELING MANIC / ELATED / WIRED	0-5							
TOOK CARE OF CHORES	Y/N							
LACK OF MOTIVATION	0-5							
ATTENDED THERAPY	Y/N							
TROUBLE SLEEPING	0-5							
SELF-CARE ACTIVITIES	Y/N							
LOGGED DIARY	Y/N							
FEELING IRRITABLE	0-5							
EXPERIENCED RELATIONSHIP PROBLEMS	Y/N							
EMOTIONAL NUMBNESS	0-5							
ENGAGED IN SOCIAL ACTIVITIES	Y/N							
SELF ESTEEM	0-5							
USED COPING SKILLS	Y/N							

USE THIS CHART TO TRACK DAILY MOODS, SYMPTOMS AND HABITS. KEEP AN EYE IF THINGS CHANGE AND HOW YOU FEEL AFTER MAKING POSITIVE STEPS.

DID MENTAL HEALTH AND SYMPTOM CHECK LIST

	FREQ. / SEVERITY Y/N	MON	TUES	WED	THURS	FRI	SAT	SUN
EXERCISE	MINS							
FEELING CALM	0-5							
FEELING HAPPY	0-5							
FEELING PRODUCTIVE	0-5							
WORK/SCHOOL STRESS	0-5							
GENERAL STRESS	0-5							
SPOKE TO SOMEONE ABOUT FEELINGS	Y/N							
MEDICATION	DOSE							
MEDICATION	DOSE							
MEDICATION	DOSE							
MEDICATION	DOSE							
MEDICATION	DOSE							

FILL IN THE CHARTS TO TRACK EVENTS, MOODS, TRIGGERS, HOW ALTERS AND THE SYSTEM COPED, THINGS YOU WANT TO CHANGE, HABITS YOUR SYSTEM IS TRYING TO IMPLEMENT ETC.

_____
_____
_____
_____
_____
_____
_____
_____
_____
_____
_____
_____

HOW OFTEN WAS THIS CHART FILLED OUT?
NOT AT ALL [ ]   1-3X PER WEEK [ ]   ALMOST EVERY DAY [ ]   EVERYDAY [ ]

DAILY ENERGY vs MOOD TRACKER

TRACK YOUR DAILY ENERGY AND MOOD USING DIFFERENT COLOURS ON THIS LINE CHART - NOTE YOUR TRIGGERS BELOW.

100

75

50

25

0

ENERGY MONDAY   TUESDAY   WEDNESDAY   THURSDAY   FRIDAY   SATURDAY   SUNDAY   MOOD

DID MENTAL HEALTH AND SYMPTOM CHECK LIST   NAME_____ DATE_____

	FREQ. / SEVERITY Y/N	MON	TUES	WED	THURS	FRI	SAT	SUN
OVERALL MOOD	0-5							
ENERGY LEVELS	0-5							
ANXIETY	0-5							
AMNESIA / MEMORY PROBLEMS	Y/N							
RANDOM SWITCH	Y/N							
TRIGGERED SWITCH	Y/N							
DEPRESSION	0-5							
LOTS OF SWITCHING	Y/N							
"EMOTIONAL HANGOVER"	Y/N							
RAPID CYCLING MOOD SWINGS	Y/N							
FEELING OVERWHELMED	0-5							
FEELING MANIC / ELATED / WIRED	0-5							
TOOK CARE OF CHORES	Y/N							
LACK OF MOTIVATION	0-5							
ATTENDED THERAPY	Y/N							
TROUBLE SLEEPING	0-5							
SELF-CARE ACTIVITIES	Y/N							
LOGGED DIARY	Y/N							
FEELING IRRITABLE	0-5							
EXPERIENCED RELATIONSHIP PROBLEMS	Y/N							
EMOTIONAL NUMBNESS	0-5							
ENGAGED IN SOCIAL ACTIVITIES	Y/N							
SELF ESTEEM	0-5							
USED COPING SKILLS	Y/N							

USE THIS CHART TO TRACK DAILY MOODS, SYMPTOMS AND HABITS. KEEP AN EYE IF THINGS CHANGE AND HOW YOU FEEL AFTER MAKING POSITIVE STEPS.

DID MENTAL HEALTH AND SYMPTOM CHECK LIST

	FREQ. / SEVERITY Y/N	MON	TUES	WED	THURS	FRI	SAT	SUN
EXERCISE	MINS							
FEELING CALM	0-5							
FEELING HAPPY	0-5							
FEELING PRODUCTIVE	0-5							
WORK/SCHOOL STRESS	0-5							
GENERAL STRESS	0-5							
SPOKE TO SOMEONE ABOUT FEELINGS	Y/N							
MEDICATION	DOSE							
MEDICATION	DOSE							
MEDICATION	DOSE							
MEDICATION	DOSE							
MEDICATION	DOSE							

FILL IN THE CHARTS TO TRACK EVENTS, MOODS, TRIGGERS, HOW ALTERS AND THE SYSTEM COPED, THINGS YOU WANT TO CHANGE, HABITS YOUR SYSTEM IS TRYING TO IMPLEMENT ETC.

_____
_____
_____
_____
_____
_____
_____
_____
_____
_____
_____
_____
_____
_____

HOW OFTEN WAS THIS CHART FILLED OUT?
NOT AT ALL [ ]   1-3X PER WEEK [ ]   ALMOST EVERY DAY [ ]   EVERYDAY [ ]

DAILY ENERGY vs MOOD TRACKER

TRACK YOUR DAILY ENERGY AND MOOD USING DIFFERENT COLOURS ON THIS LINE CHART - NOTE YOUR TRIGGERS BELOW.

100

75

50

25

0

ENERGY   MONDAY   TUESDAY   WEDNESDAY   THURSDAY   FRIDAY   SATURDAY   SUNDAY   MOOD

_____
_____
_____
_____
_____
_____
_____
_____
_____
_____
_____
_____
_____
_____
_____
_____
_____
_____

DID MENTAL HEALTH AND SYMPTOM CHECK LIST   NAME_____ DATE____

	FREQ. / SEVERITY Y/N	MON	TUES	WED	THURS	FRI	SAT	SUN
OVERALL MOOD	0-5							
ENERGY LEVELS	0-5							
ANXIETY	0-5							
AMNESIA / MEMORY PROBLEMS	Y/N							
RANDOM SWITCH	Y/N							
TRIGGERED SWITCH	Y/N							
DEPRESSION	0-5							
LOTS OF SWITCHING	Y/N							
"EMOTIONAL HANGOVER"	Y/N							
RAPID CYCLING MOOD SWINGS	Y/N							
FEELING OVERWHELMED	0-5							
FEELING MANIC / ELATED / WIRED	0-5							
TOOK CARE OF CHORES	Y/N							
LACK OF MOTIVATION	0-5							
ATTENDED THERAPY	Y/N							
TROUBLE SLEEPING	0-5							
SELF-CARE ACTIVITIES	Y/N							
LOGGED DIARY	Y/N							
FEELING IRRITABLE	0-5							
EXPERIENCED RELATIONSHIP PROBLEMS	Y/N							
EMOTIONAL NUMBNESS	0-5							
ENGAGED IN SOCIAL ACTIVITIES	Y/N							
SELF ESTEEM	0-5							
USED COPING SKILLS	Y/N							

USE THIS CHART TO TRACK DAILY MOODS, SYMPTOMS AND HABITS. KEEP AN EYE IF THINGS CHANGE AND HOW YOU FEEL AFTER MAKING POSITIVE STEPS.

DID MENTAL HEALTH AND SYMPTOM CHECK LIST

	FREQ. / SEVERITY Y/N	MON	TUES	WED	THURS	FRI	SAT	SUN
EXERCISE	MINS							
FEELING CALM	0-5							
FEELING HAPPY	0-5							
FEELING PRODUCTIVE	0-5							
WORK/SCHOOL STRESS	0-5							
GENERAL STRESS	0-5							
SPOKE TO SOMEONE ABOUT FEELINGS	Y/N							
MEDICATION	DOSE							
MEDICATION	DOSE							
MEDICATION	DOSE							
MEDICATION	DOSE							
MEDICATION	DOSE							

FILL IN THE CHARTS TO TRACK EVENTS, MOODS, TRIGGERS, HOW ALTERS AND THE SYSTEM COPED, THINGS YOU WANT TO CHANGE, HABITS YOUR SYSTEM IS TRYING TO IMPLEMENT ETC.

_____
_____
_____
_____
_____
_____
_____
_____
_____
_____
_____
_____

HOW OFTEN WAS THIS CHART FILLED OUT?
NOT AT ALL [ ]   1-3X PER WEEK [ ]   ALMOST EVERY DAY [ ]   EVERYDAY [ ]

DAILY ENERGY vs MOOD TRACKER

TRACK YOUR DAILY ENERGY AND MOOD USING DIFFERENT COLOURS ON THIS LINE CHART - NOTE YOUR TRIGGERS BELOW.

100

75

50

25

0
ENERGY   MONDAY   TUESDAY   WEDNESDAY   THURSDAY   FRIDAY   SATURDAY   SUNDAY   MOOD

_____
_____
_____
_____
_____
_____
_____
_____
_____
_____
_____
_____
_____
_____
_____
_____
_____

DID MENTAL HEALTH AND SYMPTOM CHECK LIST   NAME_____ DATE____

	FREQ. / SEVERITY Y/N	MON	TUES	WED	THURS	FRI	SAT	SUN
OVERALL MOOD	0-5							
ENERGY LEVELS	0-5							
ANXIETY	0-5							
AMNESIA / MEMORY PROBLEMS	Y/N							
RANDOM SWITCH	Y/N							
TRIGGERED SWITCH	Y/N							
DEPRESSION	0-5							
LOTS OF SWITCHING	Y/N							
"EMOTIONAL HANGOVER"	Y/N							
RAPID CYCLING MOOD SWINGS	Y/N							
FEELING OVERWHELMED	0-5							
FEELING MANIC / ELATED / WIRED	0-5							
TOOK CARE OF CHORES	Y/N							
LACK OF MOTIVATION	0-5							
ATTENDED THERAPY	Y/N							
TROUBLE SLEEPING	0-5							
SELF-CARE ACTIVITIES	Y/N							
LOGGED DIARY	Y/N							
FEELING IRRITABLE	0-5							
EXPERIENCED RELATIONSHIP PROBLEMS	Y/N							
EMOTIONAL NUMBNESS	0-5							
ENGAGED IN SOCIAL ACTIVITIES	Y/N							
SELF ESTEEM	0-5							
USED COPING SKILLS	Y/N							

USE THIS CHART TO TRACK DAILY MOODS, SYMPTOMS AND HABITS. KEEP AN EYE IF THINGS CHANGE AND HOW YOU FEEL AFTER MAKING POSITIVE STEPS.

DID MENTAL HEALTH AND SYMPTOM CHECK LIST

	FREQ. / SEVERITY Y/N	MON	TUES	WED	THURS	FRI	SAT	SUN
EXERCISE	MINS							
FEELING CALM	0-5							
FEELING HAPPY	0-5							
FEELING PRODUCTIVE	0-5							
WORK/SCHOOL STRESS	0-5							
GENERAL STRESS	0-5							
SPOKE TO SOMEONE ABOUT FEELINGS	Y/N							
MEDICATION	DOSE							
MEDICATION	DOSE							
MEDICATION	DOSE							
MEDICATION	DOSE							
MEDICATION	DOSE							

FILL IN THE CHARTS TO TRACK EVENTS, MOODS, TRIGGERS, HOW ALTERS AND THE SYSTEM COPED, THINGS YOU WANT TO CHANGE, HABITS YOUR SYSTEM IS TRYING TO IMPLEMENT ETC.

_____
_____
_____
_____
_____
_____
_____
_____
_____
_____
_____
_____
_____

HOW OFTEN WAS THIS CHART FILLED OUT?
NOT AT ALL [ ]   1-3X PER WEEK [ ]   ALMOST EVERY DAY [ ]   EVERYDAY [ ]

DAILY ENERGY vs MOOD TRACKER

TRACK YOUR DAILY ENERGY AND MOOD USING DIFFERENT COLOURS ON THIS LINE CHART - NOTE YOUR TRIGGERS BELOW.

100

75

50

25

0

ENERGY MONDAY TUESDAY WEDNESDAY THURSDAY FRIDAY SATURDAY SUNDAY MOOD

DID MENTAL HEALTH AND SYMPTOM CHECK LIST   NAME_____ DATE_____

	FREQ. / SEVERITY Y/N	MON	TUES	WED	THURS	FRI	SAT	SUN
OVERALL MOOD	0-5							
ENERGY LEVELS	0-5							
ANXIETY	0-5							
AMNESIA / MEMORY PROBLEMS	Y/N							
RANDOM SWITCH	Y/N							
TRIGGERED SWITCH	Y/N							
DEPRESSION	0-5							
LOTS OF SWITCHING	Y/N							
"EMOTIONAL HANGOVER"	Y/N							
RAPID CYCLING MOOD SWINGS	Y/N							
FEELING OVERWHELMED	0-5							
FEELING MANIC / ELATED / WIRED	0-5							
TOOK CARE OF CHORES	Y/N							
LACK OF MOTIVATION	0-5							
ATTENDED THERAPY	Y/N							
TROUBLE SLEEPING	0-5							
SELF-CARE ACTIVITIES	Y/N							
LOGGED DIARY	Y/N							
FEELING IRRITABLE	0-5							
EXPERIENCED RELATIONSHIP PROBLEMS	Y/N							
EMOTIONAL NUMBNESS	0-5							
ENGAGED IN SOCIAL ACTIVITIES	Y/N							
SELF ESTEEM	0-5							
USED COPING SKILLS	Y/N							

USE THIS CHART TO TRACK DAILY MOODS, SYMPTOMS AND HABITS. KEEP AN EYE IF THINGS CHANGE AND HOW YOU FEEL AFTER MAKING POSITIVE STEPS.

DID MENTAL HEALTH AND SYMPTOM CHECK LIST

	FREQ. / SEVERITY Y/N	MON	TUES	WED	THURS	FRI	SAT	SUN
EXERCISE	MINS							
FEELING CALM	0-5							
FEELING HAPPY	0-5							
FEELING PRODUCTIVE	0-5							
WORK/SCHOOL STRESS	0-5							
GENERAL STRESS	0-5							
SPOKE TO SOMEONE ABOUT FEELINGS	Y/N							
MEDICATION	DOSE							
MEDICATION	DOSE							
MEDICATION	DOSE							
MEDICATION	DOSE							
MEDICATION	DOSE							

FILL IN THE CHARTS TO TRACK EVENTS, MOODS, TRIGGERS, HOW ALTERS AND THE SYSTEM COPED, THINGS YOU WANT TO CHANGE, HABITS YOUR SYSTEM IS TRYING TO IMPLEMENT ETC.

_____
_____
_____
_____
_____
_____
_____
_____
_____
_____
_____
_____
_____

HOW OFTEN WAS THIS CHART FILLED OUT?
NOT AT ALL [ ]   1-3X PER WEEK [ ]   ALMOST EVERY DAY [ ]   EVERYDAY [ ]

DAILY ENERGY vs MOOD TRACKER

TRACK YOUR DAILY ENERGY AND MOOD USING DIFFERENT COLOURS ON THIS LINE CHART - NOTE YOUR TRIGGERS BELOW.

100

75

50

25

0

ENERGY   MONDAY   TUESDAY   WEDNESDAY   THURSDAY   FRIDAY   SATURDAY   SUNDAY   MOOD

DID MENTAL HEALTH AND SYMPTOM CHECK LIST   NAME_____ DATE_____

	FREQ. / SEVERITY Y/N	MON	TUES	WED	THURS	FRI	SAT	SUN
OVERALL MOOD	0-5							
ENERGY LEVELS	0-5							
ANXIETY	0-5							
AMNESIA / MEMORY PROBLEMS	Y/N							
RANDOM SWITCH	Y/N							
TRIGGERED SWITCH	Y/N							
DEPRESSION	0-5							
LOTS OF SWITCHING	Y/N							
"EMOTIONAL HANGOVER"	Y/N							
RAPID CYCLING MOOD SWINGS	Y/N							
FEELING OVERWHELMED	0-5							
FEELING MANIC / ELATED / WIRED	0-5							
TOOK CARE OF CHORES	Y/N							
LACK OF MOTIVATION	0-5							
ATTENDED THERAPY	Y/N							
TROUBLE SLEEPING	0-5							
SELF-CARE ACTIVITIES	Y/N							
LOGGED DIARY	Y/N							
FEELING IRRITABLE	0-5							
EXPERIENCED RELATIONSHIP PROBLEMS	Y/N							
EMOTIONAL NUMBNESS	0-5							
ENGAGED IN SOCIAL ACTIVITIES	Y/N							
SELF ESTEEM	0-5							
USED COPING SKILLS	Y/N							

USE THIS CHART TO TRACK DAILY MOODS, SYMPTOMS AND HABITS. KEEP AN EYE IF THINGS CHANGE AND HOW YOU FEEL AFTER MAKING POSITIVE STEPS.

DID MENTAL HEALTH AND SYMPTOM CHECK LIST

	FREQ. / SEVERITY Y/N	MON	TUES	WED	THURS	FRI	SAT	SUN
EXERCISE	MINS							
FEELING CALM	0-5							
FEELING HAPPY	0-5							
FEELING PRODUCTIVE	0-5							
WORK/SCHOOL STRESS	0-5							
GENERAL STRESS	0-5							
SPOKE TO SOMEONE ABOUT FEELINGS	Y/N							
MEDICATION	DOSE							
MEDICATION	DOSE							
MEDICATION	DOSE							
MEDICATION	DOSE							
MEDICATION	DOSE							

FILL IN THE CHARTS TO TRACK EVENTS, MOODS, TRIGGERS, HOW ALTERS AND THE SYSTEM COPED, THINGS YOU WANT TO CHANGE, HABITS YOUR SYSTEM IS TRYING TO IMPLEMENT ETC.

_____
_____
_____
_____
_____
_____
_____
_____
_____
_____
_____
_____

HOW OFTEN WAS THIS CHART FILLED OUT?
NOT AT ALL [ ]   1-3X PER WEEK [ ]   ALMOST EVERY DAY [ ]   EVERYDAY [ ]

DAILY ENERGY vs MOOD TRACKER

TRACK YOUR DAILY ENERGY AND MOOD USING DIFFERENT COLOURS ON THIS LINE CHART - NOTE YOUR TRIGGERS BELOW.

100

75

50

25

0

ENERGY MONDAY   TUESDAY   WEDNESDAY   THURSDAY   FRIDAY   SATURDAY   SUNDAY   MOOD

DID MENTAL HEALTH AND SYMPTOM CHECK LIST   NAME_____ DATE____

	FREQ. / SEVERITY Y/N	MON	TUES	WED	THURS	FRI	SAT	SUN
OVERALL MOOD	0-5							
ENERGY LEVELS	0-5							
ANXIETY	0-5							
AMNESIA / MEMORY PROBLEMS	Y/N							
RANDOM SWITCH	Y/N							
TRIGGERED SWITCH	Y/N							
DEPRESSION	0-5							
LOTS OF SWITCHING	Y/N							
"EMOTIONAL HANGOVER"	Y/N							
RAPID CYCLING MOOD SWINGS	Y/N							
FEELING OVERWHELMED	0-5							
FEELING MANIC / ELATED / WIRED	0-5							
TOOK CARE OF CHORES	Y/N							
LACK OF MOTIVATION	0-5							
ATTENDED THERAPY	Y/N							
TROUBLE SLEEPING	0-5							
SELF-CARE ACTIVITIES	Y/N							
LOGGED DIARY	Y/N							
FEELING IRRITABLE	0-5							
EXPERIENCED RELATIONSHIP PROBLEMS	Y/N							
EMOTIONAL NUMBNESS	0-5							
ENGAGED IN SOCIAL ACTIVITIES	Y/N							
SELF ESTEEM	0-5							
USED COPING SKILLS	Y/N							

USE THIS CHART TO TRACK DAILY MOODS, SYMPTOMS AND HABITS. KEEP AN EYE IF THINGS CHANGE AND HOW YOU FEEL AFTER MAKING POSITIVE STEPS.

DID MENTAL HEALTH AND SYMPTOM CHECK LIST

	FREQ. / SEVERITY Y/N	MON	TUES	WED	THURS	FRI	SAT	SUN
EXERCISE	MINS							
FEELING CALM	0-5							
FEELING HAPPY	0-5							
FEELING PRODUCTIVE	0-5							
WORK/SCHOOL STRESS	0-5							
GENERAL STRESS	0-5							
SPOKE TO SOMEONE ABOUT FEELINGS	Y/N							
MEDICATION	DOSE							
MEDICATION	DOSE							
MEDICATION	DOSE							
MEDICATION	DOSE							
MEDICATION	DOSE							

FILL IN THE CHARTS TO TRACK EVENTS, MOODS, TRIGGERS, HOW ALTERS AND THE SYSTEM COPED, THINGS YOU WANT TO CHANGE, HABITS YOUR SYSTEM IS TRYING TO IMPLEMENT ETC.

_____
_____
_____
_____
_____
_____
_____
_____
_____
_____
_____
_____
_____
_____

HOW OFTEN WAS THIS CHART FILLED OUT?
NOT AT ALL   [ ]   1-3X PER WEEK   [ ]   ALMOST EVERY DAY   [ ]   EVERYDAY   [ ]

DAILY ENERGY vs MOOD TRACKER

TRACK YOUR DAILY ENERGY AND MOOD USING DIFFERENT COLOURS ON THIS LINE CHART - NOTE YOUR TRIGGERS BELOW.

100

75

50

25

0
ENERGY | MONDAY | TUESDAY | WEDNESDAY | THURSDAY | FRIDAY | SATURDAY | SUNDAY | MOOD

DID MENTAL HEALTH AND SYMPTOM CHECK LIST   NAME_____ DATE____

	FREQ. / SEVERITY Y/N	MON	TUES	WED	THURS	FRI	SAT	SUN
OVERALL MOOD	0-5							
ENERGY LEVELS	0-5							
ANXIETY	0-5							
AMNESIA / MEMORY PROBLEMS	Y/N							
RANDOM SWITCH	Y/N							
TRIGGERED SWITCH	Y/N							
DEPRESSION	0-5							
LOTS OF SWITCHING	Y/N							
"EMOTIONAL HANGOVER"	Y/N							
RAPID CYCLING MOOD SWINGS	Y/N							
FEELING OVERWHELMED	0-5							
FEELING MANIC / ELATED / WIRED	0-5							
TOOK CARE OF CHORES	Y/N							
LACK OF MOTIVATION	0-5							
ATTENDED THERAPY	Y/N							
TROUBLE SLEEPING	0-5							
SELF-CARE ACTIVITIES	Y/N							
LOGGED DIARY	Y/N							
FEELING IRRITABLE	0-5							
EXPERIENCED RELATIONSHIP PROBLEMS	Y/N							
EMOTIONAL NUMBNESS	0-5							
ENGAGED IN SOCIAL ACTIVITIES	Y/N							
SELF ESTEEM	0-5							
USED COPING SKILLS	Y/N							

USE THIS CHART TO TRACK DAILY MOODS, SYMPTOMS AND HABITS. KEEP AN EYE IF THINGS CHANGE AND HOW YOU FEEL AFTER MAKING POSITIVE STEPS.

DID MENTAL HEALTH AND SYMPTOM CHECK LIST

	FREQ. / SEVERITY Y/N	MON	TUES	WED	THURS	FRI	SAT	SUN
EXERCISE	MINS							
FEELING CALM	0-5							
FEELING HAPPY	0-5							
FEELING PRODUCTIVE	0-5							
WORK/SCHOOL STRESS	0-5							
GENERAL STRESS	0-5							
SPOKE TO SOMEONE ABOUT FEELINGS	Y/N							
MEDICATION	DOSE							
MEDICATION	DOSE							
MEDICATION	DOSE							
MEDICATION	DOSE							
MEDICATION	DOSE							

FILL IN THE CHARTS TO TRACK EVENTS, MOODS, TRIGGERS, HOW ALTERS AND THE SYSTEM COPED, THINGS YOU WANT TO CHANGE, HABITS YOUR SYSTEM IS TRYING TO IMPLEMENT ETC.

___
___
___
___
___
___
___
___
___
___
___
___

HOW OFTEN WAS THIS CHART FILLED OUT?
NOT AT ALL [ ]   1-3X PER WEEK [ ]   ALMOST EVERY DAY [ ]   EVERYDAY [ ]

DAILY ENERGY vs MOOD TRACKER

TRACK YOUR DAILY ENERGY AND MOOD USING DIFFERENT COLOURS ON THIS LINE CHART - NOTE YOUR TRIGGERS BELOW.

100

75

50

25

0

ENERGY | MONDAY | TUESDAY | WEDNESDAY | THURSDAY | FRIDAY | SATURDAY | SUNDAY | MOOD

DID MENTAL HEALTH AND SYMPTOM CHECK LIST   NAME_____ DATE____

	FREQ. / SEVERITY Y/N	MON	TUES	WED	THURS	FRI	SAT	SUN
OVERALL MOOD	0-5							
ENERGY LEVELS	0-5							
ANXIETY	0-5							
AMNESIA / MEMORY PROBLEMS	Y/N							
RANDOM SWITCH	Y/N							
TRIGGERED SWITCH	Y/N							
DEPRESSION	0-5							
LOTS OF SWITCHING	Y/N							
"EMOTIONAL HANGOVER"	Y/N							
RAPID CYCLING MOOD SWINGS	Y/N							
FEELING OVERWHELMED	0-5							
FEELING MANIC / ELATED / WIRED	0-5							
TOOK CARE OF CHORES	Y/N							
LACK OF MOTIVATION	0-5							
ATTENDED THERAPY	Y/N							
TROUBLE SLEEPING	0-5							
SELF-CARE ACTIVITIES	Y/N							
LOGGED DIARY	Y/N							
FEELING IRRITABLE	0-5							
EXPERIENCED RELATIONSHIP PROBLEMS	Y/N							
EMOTIONAL NUMBNESS	0-5							
ENGAGED IN SOCIAL ACTIVITIES	Y/N							
SELF ESTEEM	0-5							
USED COPING SKILLS	Y/N							

USE THIS CHART TO TRACK DAILY MOODS, SYMPTOMS AND HABITS. KEEP AN EYE IF THINGS CHANGE AND HOW YOU FEEL AFTER MAKING POSITIVE STEPS.

DID MENTAL HEALTH AND SYMPTOM CHECK LIST

	FREQ. / SEVERITY Y/N	MON	TUES	WED	THURS	FRI	SAT	SUN
EXERCISE	MINS							
FEELING CALM	0-5							
FEELING HAPPY	0-5							
FEELING PRODUCTIVE	0-5							
WORK/SCHOOL STRESS	0-5							
GENERAL STRESS	0-5							
SPOKE TO SOMEONE ABOUT FEELINGS	Y/N							
MEDICATION	DOSE							
MEDICATION	DOSE							
MEDICATION	DOSE							
MEDICATION	DOSE							
MEDICATION	DOSE							

FILL IN THE CHARTS TO TRACK EVENTS, MOODS, TRIGGERS, HOW ALTERS AND THE SYSTEM COPED, THINGS YOU WANT TO CHANGE, HABITS YOUR SYSTEM IS TRYING TO IMPLEMENT ETC.

_____
_____
_____
_____
_____
_____
_____
_____
_____
_____
_____
_____

HOW OFTEN WAS THIS CHART FILLED OUT?

NOT AT ALL [ ]   1-3X PER WEEK [ ]   ALMOST EVERY DAY [ ]   EVERYDAY [ ]

DAILY ENERGY vs MOOD TRACKER

TRACK YOUR DAILY ENERGY AND MOOD USING DIFFERENT COLOURS ON THIS LINE CHART - NOTE YOUR TRIGGERS BELOW.

100

75

50

25

0

ENERGY | MONDAY | TUESDAY | WEDNESDAY | THURSDAY | FRIDAY | SATURDAY | SUNDAY | MOOD

DID MENTAL HEALTH AND SYMPTOM CHECK LIST   NAME_____ DATE____

	FREQ. / SEVERITY Y/N	MON	TUES	WED	THURS	FRI	SAT	SUN
OVERALL MOOD	0-5							
ENERGY LEVELS	0-5							
ANXIETY	0-5							
AMNESIA / MEMORY PROBLEMS	Y/N							
RANDOM SWITCH	Y/N							
TRIGGERED SWITCH	Y/N							
DEPRESSION	0-5							
LOTS OF SWITCHING	Y/N							
"EMOTIONAL HANGOVER"	Y/N							
RAPID CYCLING MOOD SWINGS	Y/N							
FEELING OVERWHELMED	0-5							
FEELING MANIC / ELATED / WIRED	0-5							
TOOK CARE OF CHORES	Y/N							
LACK OF MOTIVATION	0-5							
ATTENDED THERAPY	Y/N							
TROUBLE SLEEPING	0-5							
SELF-CARE ACTIVITIES	Y/N							
LOGGED DIARY	Y/N							
FEELING IRRITABLE	0-5							
EXPERIENCED RELATIONSHIP PROBLEMS	Y/N							
EMOTIONAL NUMBNESS	0-5							
ENGAGED IN SOCIAL ACTIVITIES	Y/N							
SELF ESTEEM	0-5							
USED COPING SKILLS	Y/N							

USE THIS CHART TO TRACK DAILY MOODS, SYMPTOMS AND HABITS. KEEP AN EYE IF THINGS CHANGE AND HOW YOU FEEL AFTER MAKING POSITIVE STEPS.

DID MENTAL HEALTH AND SYMPTOM CHECK LIST

	FREQ. / SEVERITY Y/N	MON	TUES	WED	THURS	FRI	SAT	SUN
EXERCISE	MINS							
FEELING CALM	0-5							
FEELING HAPPY	0-5							
FEELING PRODUCTIVE	0-5							
WORK/SCHOOL STRESS	0-5							
GENERAL STRESS	0-5							
SPOKE TO SOMEONE ABOUT FEELINGS	Y/N							
MEDICATION	DOSE							
MEDICATION	DOSE							
MEDICATION	DOSE							
MEDICATION	DOSE							
MEDICATION	DOSE							

FILL IN THE CHARTS TO TRACK EVENTS, MOODS, TRIGGERS, HOW ALTERS AND THE SYSTEM COPED, THINGS YOU WANT TO CHANGE, HABITS YOUR SYSTEM IS TRYING TO IMPLEMENT ETC.

_____
_____
_____
_____
_____
_____
_____
_____
_____
_____
_____
_____
_____

HOW OFTEN WAS THIS CHART FILLED OUT?
NOT AT ALL [ ]   1-3X PER WEEK [ ]   ALMOST EVERY DAY [ ]   EVERYDAY [ ]

DAILY ENERGY vs MOOD TRACKER

TRACK YOUR DAILY ENERGY AND MOOD USING DIFFERENT COLOURS ON THIS LINE CHART - NOTE YOUR TRIGGERS BELOW.

100							
75							
50							
25							
0	MONDAY	TUESDAY	WEDNESDAY	THURSDAY	FRIDAY	SATURDAY	SUNDAY

ENERGY   MOOD

DID MENTAL HEALTH AND SYMPTOM CHECK LIST   NAME_____ DATE_____

	FREQ. / SEVERITY Y/N	MON	TUES	WED	THURS	FRI	SAT	SUN
OVERALL MOOD	0-5							
ENERGY LEVELS	0-5							
ANXIETY	0-5							
AMNESIA / MEMORY PROBLEMS	Y/N							
RANDOM SWITCH	Y/N							
TRIGGERED SWITCH	Y/N							
DEPRESSION	0-5							
LOTS OF SWITCHING	Y/N							
"EMOTIONAL HANGOVER"	Y/N							
RAPID CYCLING MOOD SWINGS	Y/N							
FEELING OVERWHELMED	0-5							
FEELING MANIC / ELATED / WIRED	0-5							
TOOK CARE OF CHORES	Y/N							
LACK OF MOTIVATION	0-5							
ATTENDED THERAPY	Y/N							
TROUBLE SLEEPING	0-5							
SELF-CARE ACTIVITIES	Y/N							
LOGGED DIARY	Y/N							
FEELING IRRITABLE	0-5							
EXPERIENCED RELATIONSHIP PROBLEMS	Y/N							
EMOTIONAL NUMBNESS	0-5							
ENGAGED IN SOCIAL ACTIVITIES	Y/N							
SELF ESTEEM	0-5							
USED COPING SKILLS	Y/N							

USE THIS CHART TO TRACK DAILY MOODS, SYMPTOMS AND HABITS. KEEP AN EYE IF THINGS CHANGE AND HOW YOU FEEL AFTER MAKING POSITIVE STEPS.

DID MENTAL HEALTH AND SYMPTOM CHECK LIST

	FREQ. / SEVERITY Y/N	MON	TUES	WED	THURS	FRI	SAT	SUN
EXERCISE	MINS							
FEELING CALM	0-5							
FEELING HAPPY	0-5							
FEELING PRODUCTIVE	0-5							
WORK/SCHOOL STRESS	0-5							
GENERAL STRESS	0-5							
SPOKE TO SOMEONE ABOUT FEELINGS	Y/N							
MEDICATION	DOSE							
MEDICATION	DOSE							
MEDICATION	DOSE							
MEDICATION	DOSE							
MEDICATION	DOSE							

FILL IN THE CHARTS TO TRACK EVENTS, MOODS, TRIGGERS, HOW ALTERS AND THE SYSTEM COPED, THINGS YOU WANT TO CHANGE, HABITS YOUR SYSTEM IS TRYING TO IMPLEMENT ETC.

_____
_____
_____
_____
_____
_____
_____
_____
_____
_____
_____
_____
_____
_____

HOW OFTEN WAS THIS CHART FILLED OUT?
NOT AT ALL [ ]   1-3X PER WEEK [ ]   ALMOST EVERY DAY [ ]   EVERYDAY [ ]

DAILY ENERGY vs MOOD TRACKER

TRACK YOUR DAILY ENERGY AND MOOD USING DIFFERENT COLOURS ON THIS LINE CHART - NOTE YOUR TRIGGERS BELOW.

100

75

50

25

0

ENERGY   MONDAY   TUESDAY   WEDNESDAY   THURSDAY   FRIDAY   SATURDAY   SUNDAY   MOOD

DID MENTAL HEALTH AND SYMPTOM CHECK LIST   NAME_____ DATE_____

	FREQ. / SEVERITY Y/N	MON	TUES	WED	THURS	FRI	SAT	SUN
OVERALL MOOD	0-5							
ENERGY LEVELS	0-5							
ANXIETY	0-5							
AMNESIA / MEMORY PROBLEMS	Y/N							
RANDOM SWITCH	Y/N							
TRIGGERED SWITCH	Y/N							
DEPRESSION	0-5							
LOTS OF SWITCHING	Y/N							
"EMOTIONAL HANGOVER"	Y/N							
RAPID CYCLING MOOD SWINGS	Y/N							
FEELING OVERWHELMED	0-5							
FEELING MANIC / ELATED / WIRED	0-5							
TOOK CARE OF CHORES	Y/N							
LACK OF MOTIVATION	0-5							
ATTENDED THERAPY	Y/N							
TROUBLE SLEEPING	0-5							
SELF-CARE ACTIVITIES	Y/N							
LOGGED DIARY	Y/N							
FEELING IRRITABLE	0-5							
EXPERIENCED RELATIONSHIP PROBLEMS	Y/N							
EMOTIONAL NUMBNESS	0-5							
ENGAGED IN SOCIAL ACTIVITIES	Y/N							
SELF ESTEEM	0-5							
USED COPING SKILLS	Y/N							

USE THIS CHART TO TRACK DAILY MOODS, SYMPTOMS AND HABITS. KEEP AN EYE IF THINGS CHANGE AND HOW YOU FEEL AFTER MAKING POSITIVE STEPS.

DID MENTAL HEALTH AND SYMPTOM CHECK LIST

	FREQ. / SEVERITY Y/N	MON	TUES	WED	THURS	FRI	SAT	SUN
EXERCISE	MINS							
FEELING CALM	0-5							
FEELING HAPPY	0-5							
FEELING PRODUCTIVE	0-5							
WORK/SCHOOL STRESS	0-5							
GENERAL STRESS	0-5							
SPOKE TO SOMEONE ABOUT FEELINGS	Y/N							
MEDICATION	DOSE							
MEDICATION	DOSE							
MEDICATION	DOSE							
MEDICATION	DOSE							
MEDICATION	DOSE							

FILL IN THE CHARTS TO TRACK EVENTS, MOODS, TRIGGERS, HOW ALTERS AND THE SYSTEM COPED, THINGS YOU WANT TO CHANGE, HABITS YOUR SYSTEM IS TRYING TO IMPLEMENT ETC.

_____
_____
_____
_____
_____
_____
_____
_____
_____
_____
_____
_____
_____

HOW OFTEN WAS THIS CHART FILLED OUT?
NOT AT ALL [ ]   1-3X PER WEEK [ ]   ALMOST EVERY DAY [ ]   EVERYDAY [ ]

DAILY ENERGY vs MOOD TRACKER

TRACK YOUR DAILY ENERGY AND MOOD USING DIFFERENT COLOURS ON THIS LINE CHART - NOTE YOUR TRIGGERS BELOW.

100

75

50

25

0   MONDAY   TUESDAY   WEDNESDAY   THURSDAY   FRIDAY   SATURDAY   SUNDAY

ENERGY   MOOD

___

___

___

___

___

___

___

___

___

___

___

___

___

___

___

___

___

___

___

___

DID MENTAL HEALTH AND SYMPTOM CHECK LIST   NAME_____ DATE_____

	FREQ. / SEVERITY Y/N	MON	TUES	WED	THURS	FRI	SAT	SUN
OVERALL MOOD	0-5							
ENERGY LEVELS	0-5							
ANXIETY	0-5							
AMNESIA / MEMORY PROBLEMS	Y/N							
RANDOM SWITCH	Y/N							
TRIGGERED SWITCH	Y/N							
DEPRESSION	0-5							
LOTS OF SWITCHING	Y/N							
"EMOTIONAL HANGOVER"	Y/N							
RAPID CYCLING MOOD SWINGS	Y/N							
FEELING OVERWHELMED	0-5							
FEELING MANIC / ELATED / WIRED	0-5							
TOOK CARE OF CHORES	Y/N							
LACK OF MOTIVATION	0-5							
ATTENDED THERAPY	Y/N							
TROUBLE SLEEPING	0-5							
SELF-CARE ACTIVITIES	Y/N							
LOGGED DIARY	Y/N							
FEELING IRRITABLE	0-5							
EXPERIENCED RELATIONSHIP PROBLEMS	Y/N							
EMOTIONAL NUMBNESS	0-5							
ENGAGED IN SOCIAL ACTIVITIES	Y/N							
SELF ESTEEM	0-5							
USED COPING SKILLS	Y/N							

USE THIS CHART TO TRACK DAILY MOODS, SYMPTOMS AND HABITS. KEEP AN EYE IF THINGS CHANGE AND HOW YOU FEEL AFTER MAKING POSITIVE STEPS.

DID MENTAL HEALTH AND SYMPTOM CHECK LIST

	FREQ. / SEVERITY Y/N	MON	TUES	WED	THURS	FRI	SAT	SUN
EXERCISE	MINS							
FEELING CALM	0-5							
FEELING HAPPY	0-5							
FEELING PRODUCTIVE	0-5							
WORK/SCHOOL STRESS	0-5							
GENERAL STRESS	0-5							
SPOKE TO SOMEONE ABOUT FEELINGS	Y/N							
MEDICATION	DOSE							
MEDICATION	DOSE							
MEDICATION	DOSE							
MEDICATION	DOSE							
MEDICATION	DOSE							

FILL IN THE CHARTS TO TRACK EVENTS, MOODS, TRIGGERS, HOW ALTERS AND THE SYSTEM COPED, THINGS YOU WANT TO CHANGE, HABITS YOUR SYSTEM IS TRYING TO IMPLEMENT ETC.

_____
_____
_____
_____
_____
_____
_____
_____
_____
_____
_____
_____

HOW OFTEN WAS THIS CHART FILLED OUT?
NOT AT ALL   [ ]   1-3X PER WEEK   [ ]   ALMOST EVERY DAY   [ ]   EVERYDAY   [ ]

DAILY ENERGY vs MOOD TRACKER

TRACK YOUR DAILY ENERGY AND MOOD USING DIFFERENT COLOURS ON THIS LINE CHART - NOTE YOUR TRIGGERS BELOW.

100

75

50

25

0

ENERGY MONDAY TUESDAY WEDNESDAY THURSDAY FRIDAY SATURDAY SUNDAY MOOD

DID MENTAL HEALTH AND SYMPTOM CHECK LIST   NAME_____ DATE_____

	FREQ. / SEVERITY Y/N	MON	TUES	WED	THURS	FRI	SAT	SUN
OVERALL MOOD	0-5							
ENERGY LEVELS	0-5							
ANXIETY	0-5							
AMNESIA / MEMORY PROBLEMS	Y/N							
RANDOM SWITCH	Y/N							
TRIGGERED SWITCH	Y/N							
DEPRESSION	0-5							
LOTS OF SWITCHING	Y/N							
"EMOTIONAL HANGOVER"	Y/N							
RAPID CYCLING MOOD SWINGS	Y/N							
FEELING OVERWHELMED	0-5							
FEELING MANIC / ELATED / WIRED	0-5							
TOOK CARE OF CHORES	Y/N							
LACK OF MOTIVATION	0-5							
ATTENDED THERAPY	Y/N							
TROUBLE SLEEPING	0-5							
SELF-CARE ACTIVITIES	Y/N							
LOGGED DIARY	Y/N							
FEELING IRRITABLE	0-5							
EXPERIENCED RELATIONSHIP PROBLEMS	Y/N							
EMOTIONAL NUMBNESS	0-5							
ENGAGED IN SOCIAL ACTIVITIES	Y/N							
SELF ESTEEM	0-5							
USED COPING SKILLS	Y/N							

USE THIS CHART TO TRACK DAILY MOODS, SYMPTOMS AND HABITS. KEEP AN EYE IF THINGS CHANGE AND HOW YOU FEEL AFTER MAKING POSITIVE STEPS.

DID MENTAL HEALTH AND SYMPTOM CHECK LIST

	FREQ. / SEVERITY Y/N	MON	TUES	WED	THURS	FRI	SAT	SUN
EXERCISE	MINS							
FEELING CALM	0-5							
FEELING HAPPY	0-5							
FEELING PRODUCTIVE	0-5							
WORK/SCHOOL STRESS	0-5							
GENERAL STRESS	0-5							
SPOKE TO SOMEONE ABOUT FEELINGS	Y/N							
MEDICATION	DOSE							
MEDICATION	DOSE							
MEDICATION	DOSE							
MEDICATION	DOSE							
MEDICATION	DOSE							

FILL IN THE CHARTS TO TRACK EVENTS, MOODS, TRIGGERS, HOW ALTERS AND THE SYSTEM COPED, THINGS YOU WANT TO CHANGE, HABITS YOUR SYSTEM IS TRYING TO IMPLEMENT ETC.

_____
_____
_____
_____
_____
_____
_____
_____
_____
_____
_____
_____
_____
_____

HOW OFTEN WAS THIS CHART FILLED OUT?
NOT AT ALL [ ]   1-3X PER WEEK [ ]   ALMOST EVERY DAY [ ]   EVERYDAY [ ]

DAILY ENERGY vs MOOD TRACKER

TRACK YOUR DAILY ENERGY AND MOOD USING DIFFERENT COLOURS ON THIS LINE CHART - NOTE YOUR TRIGGERS BELOW.

100

75

50

25

0

ENERGY   MONDAY   TUESDAY   WEDNESDAY   THURSDAY   FRIDAY   SATURDAY   SUNDAY   MOOD

DID MENTAL HEALTH AND SYMPTOM CHECK LIST   NAME_____ DATE____

	FREQ. / SEVERITY Y/N	MON	TUES	WED	THURS	FRI	SAT	SUN
OVERALL MOOD	0-5							
ENERGY LEVELS	0-5							
ANXIETY	0-5							
AMNESIA / MEMORY PROBLEMS	Y/N							
RANDOM SWITCH	Y/N							
TRIGGERED SWITCH	Y/N							
DEPRESSION	0-5							
LOTS OF SWITCHING	Y/N							
"EMOTIONAL HANGOVER"	Y/N							
RAPID CYCLING MOOD SWINGS	Y/N							
FEELING OVERWHELMED	0-5							
FEELING MANIC / ELATED / WIRED	0-5							
TOOK CARE OF CHORES	Y/N							
LACK OF MOTIVATION	0-5							
ATTENDED THERAPY	Y/N							
TROUBLE SLEEPING	0-5							
SELF-CARE ACTIVITIES	Y/N							
LOGGED DIARY	Y/N							
FEELING IRRITABLE	0-5							
EXPERIENCED RELATIONSHIP PROBLEMS	Y/N							
EMOTIONAL NUMBNESS	0-5							
ENGAGED IN SOCIAL ACTIVITIES	Y/N							
SELF ESTEEM	0-5							
USED COPING SKILLS	Y/N							

USE THIS CHART TO TRACK DAILY MOODS, SYMPTOMS AND HABITS. KEEP AN EYE IF THINGS CHANGE AND HOW YOU FEEL AFTER MAKING POSITIVE STEPS.

DID MENTAL HEALTH AND SYMPTOM CHECK LIST

	FREQ. / SEVERITY Y/N	MON	TUES	WED	THURS	FRI	SAT	SUN
EXERCISE	MINS							
FEELING CALM	0-5							
FEELING HAPPY	0-5							
FEELING PRODUCTIVE	0-5							
WORK/SCHOOL STRESS	0-5							
GENERAL STRESS	0-5							
SPOKE TO SOMEONE ABOUT FEELINGS	Y/N							
MEDICATION	DOSE							
MEDICATION	DOSE							
MEDICATION	DOSE							
MEDICATION	DOSE							
MEDICATION	DOSE							

FILL IN THE CHARTS TO TRACK EVENTS, MOODS, TRIGGERS, HOW ALTERS AND THE SYSTEM COPED, THINGS YOU WANT TO CHANGE, HABITS YOUR SYSTEM IS TRYING TO IMPLEMENT ETC.

_____
_____
_____
_____
_____
_____
_____
_____
_____
_____
_____
_____
_____

HOW OFTEN WAS THIS CHART FILLED OUT?

NOT AT ALL [ ]   1-3X PER WEEK [ ]   ALMOST EVERY DAY [ ]   EVERYDAY [ ]

DAILY ENERGY vs MOOD TRACKER

TRACK YOUR DAILY ENERGY AND MOOD USING DIFFERENT COLOURS ON THIS LINE CHART - NOTE YOUR TRIGGERS BELOW.

100

75

50

25

0
ENERGY   MONDAY   TUESDAY   WEDNESDAY   THURSDAY   FRIDAY   SATURDAY   SUNDAY   MOOD

DID MENTAL HEALTH AND SYMPTOM CHECK LIST   NAME_____ DATE_____

	FREQ. / SEVERITY Y/N	MON	TUES	WED	THURS	FRI	SAT	SUN
OVERALL MOOD	0-5							
ENERGY LEVELS	0-5							
ANXIETY	0-5							
AMNESIA / MEMORY PROBLEMS	Y/N							
RANDOM SWITCH	Y/N							
TRIGGERED SWITCH	Y/N							
DEPRESSION	0-5							
LOTS OF SWITCHING	Y/N							
"EMOTIONAL HANGOVER"	Y/N							
RAPID CYCLING MOOD SWINGS	Y/N							
FEELING OVERWHELMED	0-5							
FEELING MANIC / ELATED / WIRED	0-5							
TOOK CARE OF CHORES	Y/N							
LACK OF MOTIVATION	0-5							
ATTENDED THERAPY	Y/N							
TROUBLE SLEEPING	0-5							
SELF-CARE ACTIVITIES	Y/N							
LOGGED DIARY	Y/N							
FEELING IRRITABLE	0-5							
EXPERIENCED RELATIONSHIP PROBLEMS	Y/N							
EMOTIONAL NUMBNESS	0-5							
ENGAGED IN SOCIAL ACTIVITIES	Y/N							
SELF ESTEEM	0-5							
USED COPING SKILLS	Y/N							

USE THIS CHART TO TRACK DAILY MOODS, SYMPTOMS AND HABITS. KEEP AN EYE IF THINGS CHANGE AND HOW YOU FEEL AFTER MAKING POSITIVE STEPS.

DID MENTAL HEALTH AND SYMPTOM CHECK LIST

	FREQ. / SEVERITY Y/N	MON	TUES	WED	THURS	FRI	SAT	SUN
EXERCISE	MINS							
FEELING CALM	0-5							
FEELING HAPPY	0-5							
FEELING PRODUCTIVE	0-5							
WORK/SCHOOL STRESS	0-5							
GENERAL STRESS	0-5							
SPOKE TO SOMEONE ABOUT FEELINGS	Y/N							
MEDICATION	DOSE							
MEDICATION	DOSE							
MEDICATION	DOSE							
MEDICATION	DOSE							
MEDICATION	DOSE							

FILL IN THE CHARTS TO TRACK EVENTS, MOODS, TRIGGERS, HOW ALTERS AND THE SYSTEM COPED, THINGS YOU WANT TO CHANGE, HABITS YOUR SYSTEM IS TRYING TO IMPLEMENT ETC.

_____
_____
_____
_____
_____
_____
_____
_____
_____
_____
_____
_____
_____
_____

HOW OFTEN WAS THIS CHART FILLED OUT?
NOT AT ALL [ ]   1-3X PER WEEK [ ]   ALMOST EVERY DAY [ ]   EVERYDAY [ ]

DID MENTAL HEALTH AND SYMPTOM CHECK LIST   NAME_____ DATE____

	FREQ. / SEVERITY Y/N	MON	TUES	WED	THURS	FRI	SAT	SUN
OVERALL MOOD	0-5							
ENERGY LEVELS	0-5							
ANXIETY	0-5							
AMNESIA / MEMORY PROBLEMS	Y/N							
RANDOM SWITCH	Y/N							
TRIGGERED SWITCH	Y/N							
DEPRESSION	0-5							
LOTS OF SWITCHING	Y/N							
"EMOTIONAL HANGOVER"	Y/N							
RAPID CYCLING MOOD SWINGS	Y/N							
FEELING OVERWHELMED	0-5							
FEELING MANIC / ELATED / WIRED	0-5							
TOOK CARE OF CHORES	Y/N							
LACK OF MOTIVATION	0-5							
ATTENDED THERAPY	Y/N							
TROUBLE SLEEPING	0-5							
SELF-CARE ACTIVITIES	Y/N							
LOGGED DIARY	Y/N							
FEELING IRRITABLE	0-5							
EXPERIENCED RELATIONSHIP PROBLEMS	Y/N							
EMOTIONAL NUMBNESS	0-5							
ENGAGED IN SOCIAL ACTIVITIES	Y/N							
SELF ESTEEM	0-5							
USED COPING SKILLS	Y/N							

USE THIS CHART TO TRACK DAILY MOODS, SYMPTOMS AND HABITS. KEEP AN EYE IF THINGS CHANGE AND HOW YOU FEEL AFTER MAKING POSITIVE STEPS.

DID MENTAL HEALTH AND SYMPTOM CHECK LIST

	FREQ. / SEVERITY Y/N	MON	TUES	WED	THURS	FRI	SAT	SUN
EXERCISE	MINS							
FEELING CALM	0-5							
FEELING HAPPY	0-5							
FEELING PRODUCTIVE	0-5							
WORK/SCHOOL STRESS	0-5							
GENERAL STRESS	0-5							
SPOKE TO SOMEONE ABOUT FEELINGS	Y/N							
MEDICATION	DOSE							
MEDICATION	DOSE							
MEDICATION	DOSE							
MEDICATION	DOSE							
MEDICATION	DOSE							

FILL IN THE CHARTS TO TRACK EVENTS, MOODS, TRIGGERS, HOW ALTERS AND THE SYSTEM COPED, THINGS YOU WANT TO CHANGE, HABITS YOUR SYSTEM IS TRYING TO IMPLEMENT ETC.

___
___
___
___
___
___
___
___
___
___
___
___
___
___

HOW OFTEN WAS THIS CHART FILLED OUT?
NOT AT ALL [ ] 1-3X PER WEEK [ ] ALMOST EVERY DAY [ ] EVERYDAY [ ]

DAILY ENERGY vs MOOD TRACKER

TRACK YOUR DAILY ENERGY AND MOOD USING DIFFERENT COLOURS ON THIS LINE CHART - NOTE YOUR TRIGGERS BELOW.

100

75

50

25

0

ENERGY   MONDAY   TUESDAY   WEDNESDAY   THURSDAY   FRIDAY   SATURDAY   SUNDAY   MOOD

DID MENTAL HEALTH AND SYMPTOM CHECK LIST   NAME_____ DATE____

	FREQ. / SEVERITY Y/N	MON	TUES	WED	THURS	FRI	SAT	SUN
OVERALL MOOD	0-5							
ENERGY LEVELS	0-5							
ANXIETY	0-5							
AMNESIA / MEMORY PROBLEMS	Y/N							
RANDOM SWITCH	Y/N							
TRIGGERED SWITCH	Y/N							
DEPRESSION	0-5							
LOTS OF SWITCHING	Y/N							
"EMOTIONAL HANGOVER"	Y/N							
RAPID CYCLING MOOD SWINGS	Y/N							
FEELING OVERWHELMED	0-5							
FEELING MANIC / ELATED / WIRED	0-5							
TOOK CARE OF CHORES	Y/N							
LACK OF MOTIVATION	0-5							
ATTENDED THERAPY	Y/N							
TROUBLE SLEEPING	0-5							
SELF-CARE ACTIVITIES	Y/N							
LOGGED DIARY	Y/N							
FEELING IRRITABLE	0-5							
EXPERIENCED RELATIONSHIP PROBLEMS	Y/N							
EMOTIONAL NUMBNESS	0-5							
ENGAGED IN SOCIAL ACTIVITIES	Y/N							
SELF ESTEEM	0-5							
USED COPING SKILLS	Y/N							

USE THIS CHART TO TRACK DAILY MOODS, SYMPTOMS AND HABITS. KEEP AN EYE IF THINGS CHANGE AND HOW YOU FEEL AFTER MAKING POSITIVE STEPS.

DID MENTAL HEALTH AND SYMPTOM CHECK LIST

	FREQ. / SEVERITY Y/N	MON	TUES	WED	THURS	FRI	SAT	SUN
EXERCISE	MINS							
FEELING CALM	0-5							
FEELING HAPPY	0-5							
FEELING PRODUCTIVE	0-5							
WORK/SCHOOL STRESS	0-5							
GENERAL STRESS	0-5							
SPOKE TO SOMEONE ABOUT FEELINGS	Y/N							
MEDICATION	DOSE							
MEDICATION	DOSE							
MEDICATION	DOSE							
MEDICATION	DOSE							
MEDICATION	DOSE							

FILL IN THE CHARTS TO TRACK EVENTS, MOODS, TRIGGERS, HOW ALTERS AND THE SYSTEM COPED, THINGS YOU WANT TO CHANGE, HABITS YOUR SYSTEM IS TRYING TO IMPLEMENT ETC.

_____
_____
_____
_____
_____
_____
_____
_____
_____
_____
_____
_____

HOW OFTEN WAS THIS CHART FILLED OUT?
NOT AT ALL [ ]   1-3X PER WEEK [ ]   ALMOST EVERY DAY [ ]   EVERYDAY [ ]

DAILY ENERGY vs MOOD TRACKER

TRACK YOUR DAILY ENERGY AND MOOD USING DIFFERENT COLOURS ON THIS LINE CHART - NOTE YOUR TRIGGERS BELOW.

100

75

50

25

0

ENERGY   MONDAY   TUESDAY   WEDNESDAY   THURSDAY   FRIDAY   SATURDAY   SUNDAY   MOOD

DID MENTAL HEALTH AND SYMPTOM CHECK LIST   NAME_____ DATE_____

	FREQ. / SEVERITY Y/N	MON	TUES	WED	THURS	FRI	SAT	SUN
OVERALL MOOD	0-5							
ENERGY LEVELS	0-5							
ANXIETY	0-5							
AMNESIA / MEMORY PROBLEMS	Y/N							
RANDOM SWITCH	Y/N							
TRIGGERED SWITCH	Y/N							
DEPRESSION	0-5							
LOTS OF SWITCHING	Y/N							
"EMOTIONAL HANGOVER"	Y/N							
RAPID CYCLING MOOD SWINGS	Y/N							
FEELING OVERWHELMED	0-5							
FEELING MANIC / ELATED / WIRED	0-5							
TOOK CARE OF CHORES	Y/N							
LACK OF MOTIVATION	0-5							
ATTENDED THERAPY	Y/N							
TROUBLE SLEEPING	0-5							
SELF-CARE ACTIVITIES	Y/N							
LOGGED DIARY	Y/N							
FEELING IRRITABLE	0-5							
EXPERIENCED RELATIONSHIP PROBLEMS	Y/N							
EMOTIONAL NUMBNESS	0-5							
ENGAGED IN SOCIAL ACTIVITIES	Y/N							
SELF ESTEEM	0-5							
USED COPING SKILLS	Y/N							

USE THIS CHART TO TRACK DAILY MOODS, SYMPTOMS AND HABITS. KEEP AN EYE IF THINGS CHANGE AND HOW YOU FEEL AFTER MAKING POSITIVE STEPS.

DID MENTAL HEALTH AND SYMPTOM CHECK LIST

	FREQ. / SEVERITY Y/N	MON	TUES	WED	THURS	FRI	SAT	SUN
EXERCISE	MINS							
FEELING CALM	0-5							
FEELING HAPPY	0-5							
FEELING PRODUCTIVE	0-5							
WORK/SCHOOL STRESS	0-5							
GENERAL STRESS	0-5							
SPOKE TO SOMEONE ABOUT FEELINGS	Y/N							
MEDICATION	DOSE							
MEDICATION	DOSE							
MEDICATION	DOSE							
MEDICATION	DOSE							
MEDICATION	DOSE							

FILL IN THE CHARTS TO TRACK EVENTS, MOODS, TRIGGERS, HOW ALTERS AND THE SYSTEM COPED, THINGS YOU WANT TO CHANGE, HABITS YOUR SYSTEM IS TRYING TO IMPLEMENT ETC.

_____
_____
_____
_____
_____
_____
_____
_____
_____
_____
_____
_____

HOW OFTEN WAS THIS CHART FILLED OUT?
NOT AT ALL [ ]   1-3X PER WEEK [ ]   ALMOST EVERY DAY [ ]   EVERYDAY [ ]

Printed in Poland
by Amazon Fulfillment
Poland Sp. z o.o., Wrocław